Contents

Introduction 2

Overview 7
SEAL outcomes 8

Lessons and worksheets
   1: Making me 9
   2: My world, your world 17
   3 Changing bodies 27
   4: Firm foundations 33
   5: Marriage 39
   6: Great expectations? 45
   7: In need of restoration? 55

Summary activities 62

Optional activity
Changing bodies 65

Appendix 1: Values related questions 69

Appendix 2: Sex and Relationships
Education sample policy 73

Appendix 3: SRE: working with parents 80

Bibliography and further resources 83

Introduction

'We are all held in a loving, accepting gaze …
what difference will it make to our relationships with
others if we believe we are all held in the same loving regard?'[1]

These materials have been written in the light of appalling statistics for teenage pregnancies and rising rates of sexually transmitted infections (STIs) in young people. At present, Britain has the highest rate of teenage pregnancies in Europe, at 27 per 1000,[2] the most common STI, Chlamydia, has seen a 150% rise over the past ten years.[3]

Meanwhile the DCSF's *Sex and Relationships Education Guidance for 2010* contains clear recommendations about a needed shift in emphasis; sexuality should be taught within relationships and a diversity of beliefs and lifestyles should be explored.[4] The Children's Society have published *A Good Childhood: Searching for Values in a Competitive Age,* a report about children's contemporary experiences of growing up, which makes strong recommendations about the way sex education should be taught.[5]

Love and Sex Matters hopes to offer a path that will deliver the recommendations of the DSCF's *Sex and Relationships Education Guidance* within a framework of Christian values and is offered as a response to suggestions made in *A Good Childhood.* The emphasis in these materials is on creating dialogue through activity that will help children and young people grow in emotional articulacy and develop the self-esteem to navigate a personal life that honours both themselves and others.

'Excessive individualism …
commercial and peer pressures encourage risky lifestyles.'[6]

These materials also aim to help young people open their eyes to how media and advertising place human sexuality and relationships within the realm of consumerism, so removing the spirituality from intimacy. These lessons aim to help children and young people to reject the advertising pressures for conformity in beauty and, instead, realise their own wonder and worth as unique and beautiful people. Thus, good self-esteem is presented as a necessary foundation for building mutually satisfying and beneficial relationships. *Love and Sex Matters* also seeks to question the media representation that teenage sexual activity is, or should be, the norm.

'As sex can create human beings, sex education should be treated
with seriousness and it should centre on love and responsibility
within the context of family life.'[7]

These materials do not offer one Christian moral path, such as abstinence before marriage; however, they do seek to present that path as a positive, viable life choice and uphold the importance of marriage and family life.

In several of the lessons, students are asked to consider a variety of Christian, other faith, agnostic and atheist perspectives on issues of relationships and sexuality. They are then encouraged to use these perspectives to discuss their own ideas, with the emphasis on developing emotional articulacy.

'There is more involved than the defence of traditional family patterns – unless believers can show all of us ways of handling the education of emotion and of preparing people for adult commitment in relationships, all that will be seen is an agenda of anxiety, censoriousness and repression.'[8]

It is hoped that through these materials children and young people will be encouraged to ponder the profound significance and meaning of sex and consider the spirituality of relationships. Although this resource has been written with church schools in mind, the teaching ethic and multi-faith approach are such that it can also make a rich contribution to sex and relationships education outside this context.

At a time of changing family patterns and parental stress overload, there are many youngsters seeking the love, attention, security and identity that may not have been afforded them as a foundational experience. As a result sexual and emotional needs, love and relationships, often get confused, conflated and entangled. Many children and young people in our schools are not given the opportunity to discuss and formulate a language to articulate their feelings and needs either at home or in other contexts. They are not, therefore, being offered a safe environment in which to decide upon a meaningful sexual ethic for themselves, one that will give them the guidelines for their life. In this way, we are not protecting the young in our care and we are not helping them to live 'life in all its fullness'.

All schools, and in particular church schools, have a responsibility to love, serve and protect the children and young people they are educating. These materials seek to help children in today's world to find their own course through the smorgasbord of modern sexuality. This is offered against the backdrop of a belief in the unconditional love of God for all and the grace of God's forgiveness.

Kate Guthrie, Verity Holloway & Katy Staples
February 2010

In summary

Love and Sex Matters aims to:

- Offer exciting, fun and interactive lessons.
- Give opportunities to rehearse appropriate language and develop articulacy.
- Build self-esteem and high regard for others; in church schools this is rooted in a belief that all are loved by God.
- Uphold the sanctity of marriage, the importance of long-term relationships and stable family life.
- Offer abstinence before marriage as a valid life choice to be taken seriously while respecting people and their life choices.
- Offer views from a variety of Christian perspectives, from other faiths and from non-religious life perspectives.
- Enable children and young people to question messages in the media and advertising about body image and sexuality.
- Offer a starting point that does not assume teenage sexual activity as the norm.
- Create opportunities for children and young people to explore the deeper questions as to the meaning and significance of the sexual act in relationships.
- Invite a holistic consideration of sexuality that takes it beyond just the physical and explores the emotional, spiritual and moral aspects of sexuality: more than an exploration of bodily changes at puberty and 'how to put a condom on a banana'.
- Be realistic in understanding the raging power and force of sexuality.
- Acknowledge the complex context of the modern world in which today's children and young people find themselves.
- Be accessible to those of all faiths and none.
- Recognise each person's intrinsic worth and value.
- Allow consideration of human relationships as part of the greater love of God.
- Offer a vision of sacred committed relationships where personal and spiritual growth and mutual support can flourish.

Creating a classroom climate for good relationships and sex education

It is intended that these materials will help children and young people develop emotional articulacy and confidence in discussing relationships. They are not DVD/worksheet factual lessons although these lessons can be used in conjunction with materials such as the Channel 4 DVD *Living & Growing*, which is recommended by many local authorities.

These lessons do require teachers to be comfortable with managing discussion about matters that may be of a sensitive nature, and they are best used after appropriate training.

These are materials that seek active learning and debate and therefore could be deemed risky by some. There are teachers who may find the open discussion of issues relating to relationships and sexuality too sensitive to handle easily. Although ideally relationships are best discussed by the class teacher, it may, in certain circumstances, be appropriate to offer support and allow lessons to be taught by a member of staff more comfortable with handling sensitive issues.

Several of the lessons include a variety of opinions from religious and non-religious perspectives. They are not intended to be the definitive orthodoxy for any faith and the inclusion of the huge range of different opinions within all faiths and non-religious life perspectives has been difficult to reflect fully. The range of opinions offered is merely intended to reflect the diversity of views held by representative (fictional) young people. The aim is that children and young people will reflect on those opinions in order to help them develop their own ethics/beliefs.

It may be worth saying that opinions for discussion should be selected not only on the basis of the age of the pupils, but also on the needs of the group. We have given simpler versions of some opinion worksheets for younger children, which means that a teacher can select which will be most appropriate for a group, or even give some small groups in a class the standard worksheet, and other groups the simpler worksheet. It would still be possible to have a whole-class discussion afterwards. There are also some extension questions for abler children. Teachers can further tailor the resources for their group by limiting the number of examples, and selecting only examples from the most appropriate faith/belief perspectives.

Some classes may find issues to do with relationships and sexuality embarrassing, sensitive and very exciting! This situation can lead to defensive and heightened behaviour such as giggling, silliness or protracted silence. Strategies to cope with these behaviours need to be developed. Teachers as far as possible need to model behaviour that shows the normality of the discourse, that there is no reason to be embarrassed or silly.

Teachers may wish to establish ground rules for behaviour to ensure good sensitive listening and an appreciation of each other's ideas without criticism – however it is likely that these are already a part of the culture of the school. Teachers need to praise and value each verbal contribution made in order to encourage the more reticent to know that it is a safe space.

Handling pupil questions: teaching SRE in partnership with the home

It is important that pupils can ask questions in a safe environment – however, there is no obligation for a teacher to answer every question. Pupils may ask questions that are not relevant to the curriculum appropriate for that age group; this may be to shock or in order to gain kudos. Answering such questions may lead discussion into an inappropriate area, one that may not meet with the approval of the governing/parent body.

It is quite acceptable for a teacher to respond to an inappropriate pupil question by explaining that it addresses an issue that pupils will cover when older and suggesting that the pupil ask someone at home in the meantime.

This type of answer protects the childhood latency of pupils in the class whilst not totally quashing the enquiry, and shares the responsibility for relationships/sex education with the parents or carers.

Some schools find the use of a question box useful. Asking pupils to put their questions into a box gives teachers an opportunity to filter out the less appropriate questions before answering. Teachers can explain that they will only answer questions that are appropriate for the class. It can also be suggested that if a pupil's question is not read out and answered, the pupil can ask someone at home or speak to the teacher directly.

Child Protection

When discussing relationship and sexuality issues in the classroom, a teacher may discover the inappropriate sexualisation of a pupil, or a disclosure could be made. Staff must know the school's processes for child protection before teaching this material.

Adapting the material to your local context

Some material included is potentially very sensitive. Depending on your local context it may be that, due to the make up of your pupil/parent/governing body, it is particularly pertinent to include the teaching of a particular issue for any given year group or indeed to omit it.

1. Rowan Williams quoted in Mike Highton, *Difficult Gospel: The Theology of Rowan Williams* (SCM Press: Canterbury, 2004), p.19.
2. Dunn, J. & Layard, Richard, *A Good Childhood: Searching for Values in a Competitive Age* (Penguin: London, 2009). 'Report Summary: Friends' available online: http://www.childrenssociety.org.uk/all_about_us/how_we_do_it/the_good_childhood_inquiry/report_summaries/14748.html [accessed 17 June 2009].
3. Avert.org, STD Statistics for the UK. [online] (updated 20 February 2009) Available at http://www.avert.org/stdstatisticuk.htm [accessed 22 June 2009].
4. Sir Alasdair Macdonald, Independent Review of the Proposal to Make Personal, Social, Health and Economic (PSHE) Education Statutory (Department for Children, Schools and Families: London, 2009) Available online at: http://publications.dcsf.gov.uk/default.aspx?PageFunction= productdetails&PageMode=publications&Productid=D SCF-00495-2009& [accessed 31 January 2010].
5. Dunn & Layard, *A Good Childhood.*
6. Dunn & Layard, *A Good Childhood.* p.4.
7. Dunn & Layard, *A Good Childhood,* p.49.
8. Rowan Williams quoted in Dunn & Layard, *A Good Childhood,* p.178.
9. *The Bible,* New International version (Zondervan: Michigan, 1978), John 10:10.

Overview

Lesson	Summary	Learning Outcomes
1: Making me	Pupils will think about the factors that contribute to an identity and what makes someone valuable	• I can describe what makes me 'me'. • I can explain why all people are valuable, including me.
2. My world, your world	Pupils will think about how their lives interact with other people's lives and how this affects decision-making.	• I can explain ways in which what I do might affect other people emotionally and/or physically. • I can identify the people whose lives might be changed by what I do. • I can explain how recognising how my actions influence other people can help me make good decisions.
3. Changing bodies	Pupils will think about the physical and emotional changes that take place during puberty.	• I can describe how I will change physically and emotionally during puberty.
4. Firm foundations	Pupils will think about what provides firm foundations for a relationship and how awareness of this might affect whom they date.	• I can describe characteristics that will help build a good relationship and why these are important. • I can explain what sort of things I might look for in a friend or partner and why.
5. Marriage	Pupils will reflect on the significance and meaning of the wedding service and marriage and how these benefit the individual and the community.	• I can explain why Christians think marriage is important. • I can explain how marriage is good for relationships within the family and with the wider community.
6. Great expectations?	Pupils will think about the meaning of sex and why it is best kept for marriage or long-term relationships.	• I can explain what I think is normal sexual behaviour. • I can describe what some religions think about sex. • I can give reasons why it might be good to keep sex for marriage or a long-term, committed relationship.
7. In need of restoration?	Pupils will think about the role of forgiveness in sustaining and deepening relationships.	• I can explain why it is good to forgive people. • I can describe some situations when I think you should or should not show forgiveness and explain why.
8. Summary activities	Activities to draw course together and encourage pupils to reflect on what they have learnt.	• I can consider what makes a relationship 'life-giving' or 'life-limiting'. • I can describe actions that would make my relationships more 'life-giving'.

Social and Emotional Aspects of Learning (SEAL) outcomes

SOCIAL SKILLS	Whole course	1. Making me	2. My world, your world	3. Changing bodies	4. Firm foundations	5. Marriage	6. Great expectations?	7. In need of restoration?
Building and maintaining relationships								
39. I can communicate effectively with others, listening to what others say as well as expressing my own thoughts and feelings	(grey)	(black)		(black)				
40. I can take others' thoughts and feelings into account in how I manage my relationships			(grey)		(black)		(black)	(grey)
41. I can assess risks and consider the issues involved before making decisions about my personal relationships	(grey)		(grey)		(grey)		(black)	
Belonging to groups								
43. I can work and learn well in groups, taking on different roles, cooperating with others to achieve a joint outcome	(grey)							
44. I understand my rights and responsibilities as an individual who belongs to many different social groups, such as my friendship group, class, school, family and community	(black)		(black)			(black)		(black)
Solving problems, including interpersonal ones								
47. I can use a range of strategies to solve problems and know how to resolve conflicts with other people, such as mediation and conflict resolution								(black)
49. I have strategies for repairing damaged relationships								(grey)

(grey) Grey denotes major themes

(black) Black denotes minor themes

Making Me

In this lesson, pupils will reflect on what forms a person's identity. They will think about how the media and advertising shape our ideas about what we should be like. They will then consider a variety of religious and non-religious perspectives on human worth, before reflecting on different reasons why people feel valued. Pupils will be encouraged to think about how they can feel valuable as a person, acknowledging that a healthy self-esteem is a necessary foundation for building healthy relationships.

Learning Objectives
• Think about what forms an identity.
• Consider what makes someone valuable.

Learning Outcomes
• I can describe what makes me 'me'.
• I can explain why I am valuable.
• I can explain why all people are valuable.

Lesson Activities and Resources
• Introduction: Advertising choices (15 minutes)
        Powerpoint 1.1: *Advertising*
• Where does my worth come from? (30 minutes)
        Worksheet/powerpoint 1.2: *What makes me valuable?*
        Worksheet 1.3: *I'm valuable opinion cards*
• Plenary: What makes me me? (15 minutes)
        Worksheet 1.4: *What makes me me?*

PSHE Curriculum
This lesson covers:
1.b. Pupils should be taught to recognise their worth as individuals by identifying positive things about themselves and their achievements, seeing their mistakes, making amends and setting personal goals.
5.b. During the key stage, pupils should be taught the knowledge, skills and understanding through opportunities to feel positive about themselves.

Introduction - Advertising choices
15 minutes - Pairs/small group activity

- Put powerpoint 1.1: *Advertising* up on a screen.
- Ask pupils, in pairs or small groups, to imagine they are making an advert for t-shirts. They have to pick one man and one woman from the pictures to be in their advert.
- After 5 minutes, start class discussion off by asking some of the groups who they picked, and why. Then use the following questions to continue discussion:
  - Which of the six people are best to use in an advert for t-shirts? Why?
  - What message does advertising give about what makes a person valuable and attractive?
  - How do you think people feel if they don't look like the people in adverts and on television?
  - Does it matter if a person doesn't look like models in adverts? Does it make them any less valuable as a person?

Where does my worth come from?
30 minutes - Small group activity

Preparation: Each small group will need three different *I'm valuable cards* from worksheet 1.3: *I'm valuable opinion cards* so you may need to print out and cut up multiple worksheets. You may want to select a variety of faith perspectives appropriate for your class, rather than use all of them. Each pupil will need a copy of worksheet 1.2: *What makes me valuable?*

Part 1

Explain to the pupils that how we feel about ourselves is often affected by how other people see us. Many religions believe that we should base our worth on how God sees us because they believe that this is what really matters.

- Give each small group three different cards from worksheet 1.3: *I'm valuable opinion cards,* and a copy of worksheet 1.2: *What makes me valuable?* for each pupil.
- Project the worksheet 1.2: *What makes me valuable?* up on the board.
- Ask pupils to write the three characters' names in the Name column on worksheet 1.2. The group should look at the cards, and then decide which of the two columns the four statements for each person fit into, as shown on the powerpoint.

- Once all the groups have finished, discuss what they have found using the following questions:
    - Did any of the people believe all the same things?
    - What did everyone believe?
    - Do you agree with any of these people's beliefs?
    - Why do you agree/not agree?

Part 2

- Ask each pupil to put their own name in the Name column of the second chart. Ask them to add three things to the second column to complete the sentence 'I know I am valuable because...'
- Ask each group to share what they have put in the second column, and then decide on three group statements that can go in the third column.
- Once all groups have finished, discuss what they have decided on by asking some groups to share their group statements. See if any group statements are shared by the whole class.

Extension questions

- Society often tells us that having good looks makes you a valuable person. Why do you think this is? Why do you agree/disagree?
- Put the following statement on the board for discussion: 'Pretty/handsome people are often boring because they never have to learn how to make friends through being entertaining and funny.'

Plenary: What makes me me?
15 minutes - Individual/class activity

Preparation: Each pupil needs a copy of worksheet 1.4: *What makes me me?*

- Pupils should pick ten statements that describe what makes them who they are and write the numbers of these statements in the middle of the person.
- Encourage pupils to write their own statements where possible.
- Once they have done this, ask pupils to count up how many statements they have chosen from each group, and answer the questions at the bottom of the worksheet.
- Discussion questions:
    - Who or what makes you know you are a valuable person?
    - How can you keep on feeling good about yourself, even when bad things happen?
    - How might feeling bad about yourself affect your relationships with other people?

Worksheet 1.1: *Advertising*

1.

2.

3.

4.

5.

6.

Worksheet 1.2: *What makes me valuable?*

Everyone believes....

I believe...

Name

Everyone believes....

I believe...

I know I am valuable because...

Name

Worksheet 1.3: *I'm valuable cards*

Frank (Christian)

- I am precious because I am made in God's image.
- God loves me whatever I do.
- What you do is more important than what you look like.
- I wish I wasn't so skinny. But I know that I am OK.

Ameena (Muslim)

- Allah made me exactly how he wants me to be.
- I don't like my nose, but I know I look fine really!
- Allah is always merciful, so looks on me kindly.
- I think that what you do is more important than what you look like.

Krishna (Hindu)

- I am part of Brahman, the one God, so I must be how I am meant to be.
- This is the body and face I have been given for this lifetime, so I have to accept it and enjoy it. I think that what you do is more important than what you look like.
- I know I look fine really, but I do think my bottom is too big.

Fred (Agnostic - unsure whether there is a God)

- I do believe that everyone is of equal value, no matter what they look like.
- I think that what people do is more important than what they look like.
- I don't believe that people are made by God: we evolved.
- I've got spots but no-one else even notices, so I'm OK really.

Hari (Buddhist)

- I believe everything is always changing, so physical beauty never lasts.
- I was born with only one hand. But I know that I am OK.
- I think that what you do is more important than what you look like.
- I think that desire brings suffering, so wanting to be different will make you suffer.

Jasminder (Sikh)

- I believe that Waheguru, the one God, put his divine spark into everyone so all humans are sacred.
- I have to wear glasses because my eyesight is bad, but I know that it doesn't matter really, I am OK.
- I think that what you do is more important than what you look like.
- I believe Waheguru is kind and sees everyone as equals.

Ruth (Jew)

- G-d cares for me and has plans for my life.
- I think that what people do is more important than what they look like.
- I am made in G-d's image, so I am special.
- I would like to be taller, but I know that I am OK.

Worksheet 1.4: *What makes me me?*

Instructions
Choose 10 sentences which explain what makes you you. Include some of your own sentences by filling in the blanks. Write the numbers of these sentences in the middle of the person.

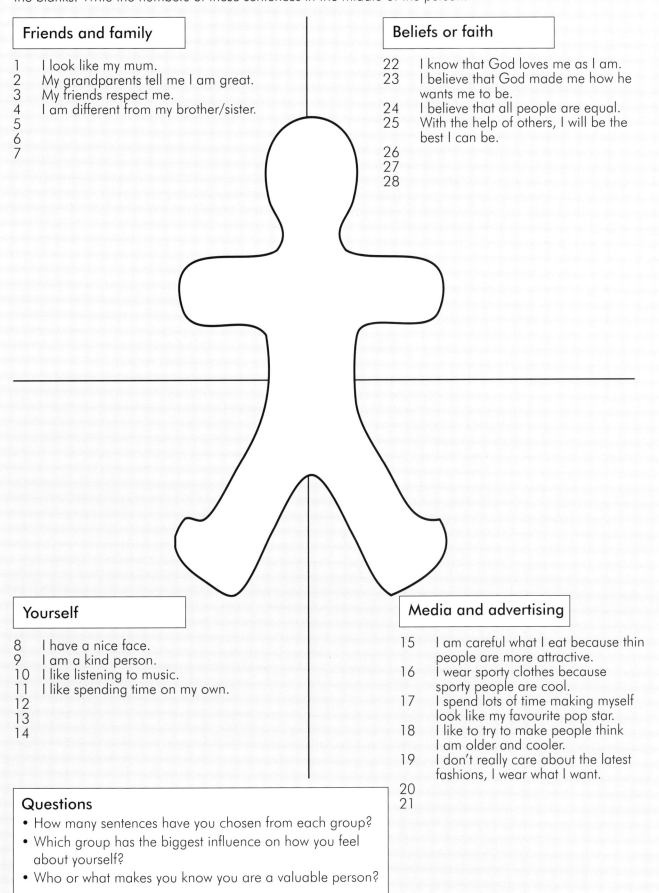

Friends and family

1   I look like my mum.
2   My grandparents tell me I am great.
3   My friends respect me.
4   I am different from my brother/sister.
5
6
7

Beliefs or faith

22   I know that God loves me as I am.
23   I believe that God made me how he wants me to be.
24   I believe that all people are equal.
25   With the help of others, I will be the best I can be.
26
27
28

Yourself

8   I have a nice face.
9   I am a kind person.
10   I like listening to music.
11   I like spending time on my own.
12
13
14

Media and advertising

15   I am careful what I eat because thin people are more attractive.
16   I wear sporty clothes because sporty people are cool.
17   I spend lots of time making myself look like my favourite pop star.
18   I like to try to make people think I am older and cooler.
19   I don't really care about the latest fashions, I wear what I want.
20
21

Questions
• How many sentences have you chosen from each group?
• Which group has the biggest influence on how you feel about yourself?
• Who or what makes you know you are a valuable person?

Lesson 2

My world, your world

In this lesson, pupils will think about how their actions can affect others both physically and emotionally. They will reflect on the possible consequences and resulting outcomes from specific decisions. They will consider how an awareness of potential consequences could guide their decision-making processes. They will be encouraged to respect others' needs and wants in making decisions and understand how this is a necessary foundation for healthy relationships.

Learning Objectives
- Understand that all actions have consequences, whether good or bad.
- Consider how our decisions can help us build good (or bad) relationships with others in our community.

Learning Outcomes
- I can describe ways in which what I do might affect other people emotionally and/or physically.
- I can identify the people whose lives might be changed by what I do.
- I can explain how recognising how my actions influence other people can help me make good decisions.

Lesson Activities and Resources
- Introduction: Actions and consequences game (15 minutes)
    Worksheet 2.1: *Actions and consequences*
- Web of consequences (30 minutes)
    Powerpoint/worksheet 2.2: *Web of consequences*
    Worksheet 2.3a/2.3b: *Blank web of consequences*
- Plenary: Life journey (15 minutes)

PSHE Curriculum
This lesson covers:
4.a. Pupils should be taught that their actions affect themselves and others, to care about other people's feelings and to try to see things from their points of view.

Lesson 2 My world, your world

Introduction - Actions and consequences game
15 minutes - Whole class activity

Preparation: Each pupil needs one card from worksheet 2.1: *Actions and consequences*. There are twenty cards on the sheet; each consequence is beside its action. If there are an odd number of pupils, give out two consequences to one of the actions.

- It may be a good idea to check that younger pupils understand the concept of 'consequences' before starting this game. Explain the meaning and ask some of them to use it in a sentence.
- Give each pupil one card. Ask them to find their other half – an action to match their consequence, or a consequence to match their action.
- When the pupils have all paired up, ask some of the pairs to read out their matching actions and consequences. If they are incorrectly matched up, then swap pairs around for next part of activity.
- In their pairs, ask pupils to think of an alternative consequence for their scenario.
- In their pairs, ask pupils to think about how the people in each scenario would feel as a result of these actions/consequences.

Web of consequences
30 minutes - Small group activity

Preparation: Each small group will need worksheet 2.3a or 2.3b: *Web of consequences*. These are two different size blank webs, so select the appropriate size for the ability of your pupils.

Part 1
5 minutes - Small group activity

- Select the most appropriate web of consequence from powerpoint 2.2: *Web of consequences* to show how any given decision can have multiple outcomes, some positive, some negative. Different outcomes will affect 'my world' and 'your world' in different ways.
- Using one of the webs, ask pupils to consider how the different people involved might feel about a given decision. What emotions will each action and consequence cause? (e.g. 'My Dad will come round to see me less' might cause emotions like 'I miss him' or 'I am sad'.)

Part 2
25 minutes - Small group activity

- In their groups, get pupils to design their own web of consequences. Each group should be given a different starting decision – either select appropriate ones from the examples below, or make up your own. Encourage the pupils to think about the emotional impact of these actions, as well as the physical impact.
    - My parents are separating – *what might the consequences be?*
    - My big sister is getting married – *what might the consequences be?*
    - I am starting at a new school on my own – *what might the consequences be?*
    - My gran is very ill so my mum has asked her to come and live with us – *what might the consequences be?*
    - My best friend is moving away – *what might the consequences be?*
    - My big brother is starting university – *what might the consequences be?*
    - My brother's seventeen-year old girlfriend is pregnant – *what might the consequences be?*
    - I have always been an only child and now my mother is having a baby – *what might the consequences be?*
    - Now that I am older my mother has decided to go back to work – *what might the consequences be?*
    - My father has taken a job in a different city – *what might the consequences be?*
- Feedback to the class, asking a few groups to present their web of consequences.
- After each group has presented their web, ask the rest of the class to suggest words that describe how the different people in the situation might feel.
- After feedback, ask the following questions to the whole class:
    - When you decide to do something, can you know what all the consequences will be? Why/why not?
    - If bad choices can have good consequences, are there any reasons for choosing to do good things?

Extension questions

- For more able pupils challenge them to see how far they can make their webs go.
- Can you think of a scenario where a decision made by one person, or a few people, has had a worldwide impact? (e.g. Mother Teresa, Mahatma Gandhi, Rosa Parks, Martin Luther King, Barack Obama, the Pope.) In what ways does this inspire you?

Plenary: Life journey
15 minutes - Individual/whole class activity

- Read one of the following poems to the class:

You ask me who I am?

I am my mother who played with me when I was little,
I am my father who abandoned us when I was five,
I am the social worker who found us a new house to live in.
I am the boys who bullied me and beat me up at school,
I am the cops who arrested me when I fought them to defend myself,
And the family of the boy I seriously injured.
I am my teacher who realised that I was struggling with life,
And the school counsellor who listened to me and cared.
I am the learning mentor who made me realise I could use my experience to help others,
I am the careers advisor who helped me find a training course,
I am the friends I made on the course, who inspired me to finish it,
And my employer, who offered me a job.
I am the youth offenders I now work with every day, helping them to deal with their anger.
I am who I am because of all these people.

You ask me who I am?

I am my mother who sang me to sleep when I was little,
I am my junior school headmistress who persuaded me to have singing lessons,
I am my music teachers who taught me to laugh at my mistakes,
I am my big sister who told me I could do it,
I am my best friend's father who drove us to rehearsals
And the man who gave up his Sunday afternoons to help us practise.
I am my friends from college who organised my first gig,
I am the old man who drove into my car on the way there,
And the young woman who stopped to help.
I am the stranger in the audience who told me to send off my CD,
And the producer who signed my contract.
I am who I am because of all these people.

- Discussion: How is the person described shaped by his/her community?

Extension questions

- Winston Churchill once said 'success is going from failure to failure without losing enthusiasm.'
  When bad things happen in life, is it possible to get something good out of them? How/why/why not?
- The poet William Ernest Henley wrote 'I am the master of my fate; I am the captain of my soul.'
  To what extent do you think you are responsible for how your life turns out?

Worksheet 2.1: *Actions and consequences*

Action:
My brother stole my sweets, so I have a tantrum.

Consequences:
My nan tells me off for having a tantrum and my brother keeps the sweets.

Action:
I ask the new kid if he/she wants to join in our game at break-time.

Consequences:
The new kid is happy because he/she has someone to play with.

Action:
I am angry because I had a bad day at school, so I talk to an adult about it.

Consequences:
I feel better because I know that someone understands that I find school hard.

Action:
I visit my grandma because she is ill.

Consequences:
Grandma feels better because she likes having visitors.

Action:
I skipped school and lied to my mum about it.

Consequences:
Mum found out I missed school and grounded me.

Action:
I get my mum some chocolates on the way home from school.

Consequences:
Mum is happy because she likes chocolate.

Action:
I make my best friend watch a film his parents don't want him to see.

Consequences:
My best friend's parents say he can't come round to my house any more because I am a bad influence.

Action:
I help an old lady cross the road.

Consequences:
The old lady is pleased because she finds crossing the road on her own hard.

Action:
I am in a rush, so I push my way to the front of the shop queue.

Consequences:
Everyone is annoyed with me for jumping the queue.

Action:
I got angry and hit my friend, so I say sorry.

Consequences:
My friend forgives me for hitting him/her, even though he/she is still hurt.

Worksheet 2.2: *Web of consequences*

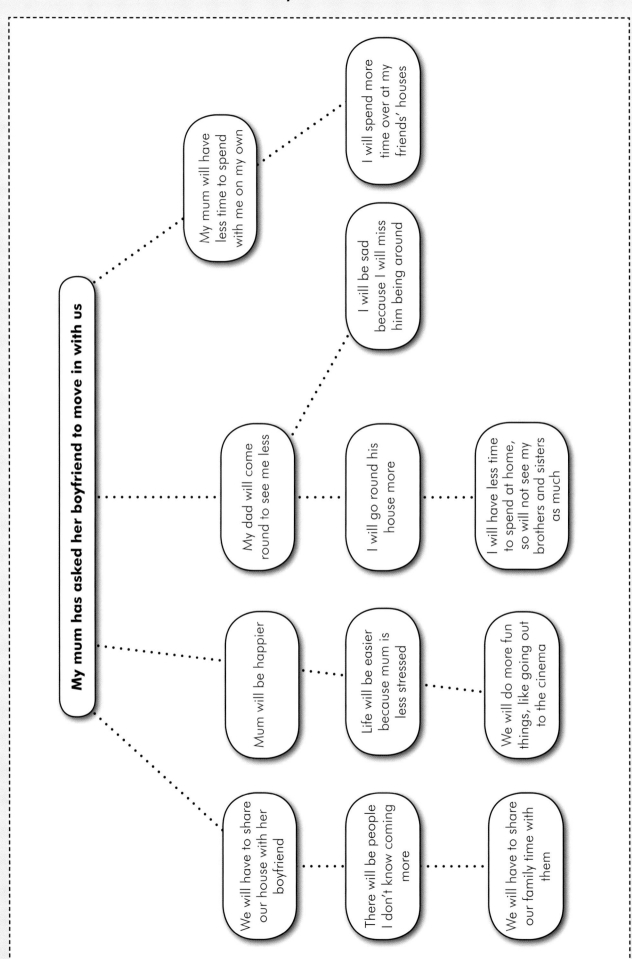

My mum has asked her boyfriend to move in with us

My mum will have less time to spend with me on my own

I will spend more time over at my friends' houses

I will be sad because I will miss him being around

My dad will come round to see me less

I will go round his house more

I will have less time to spend at home, so will not see my brothers and sisters as much

Mum will be happier

Life will be easier because mum is less stressed

We will do more fun things, like going out to the cinema

We will have to share our house with her boyfriend

There will be people I don't know coming more

We will have to share our family time with them

Worksheet 2.2: Web of consequences (cont)

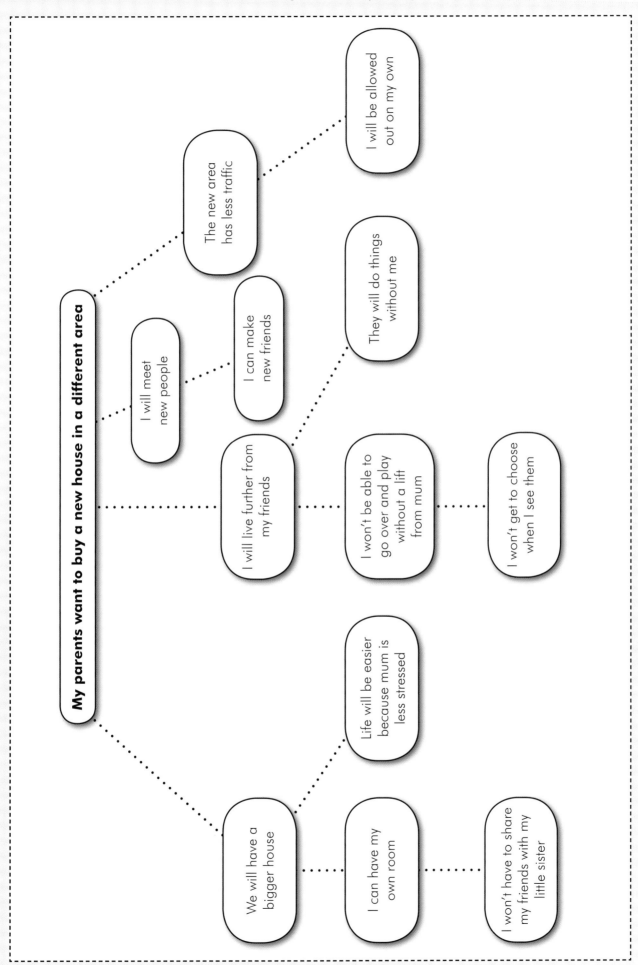

My parents want to buy a new house in a different area

- The new area has less traffic
  - I will be allowed out on my own
- I will meet new people
- I can make new friends
- They will do things without me
- I will live further from my friends
  - I won't be able to go over and play without a lift from mum
    - I won't get to choose when I see them
- We will have a bigger house
  - Life will be easier because mum is less stressed
  - I can have my own room
    - I won't have to share my friends with my little sister

Worksheet 2.3a: *Blank web of consequences*

Worksheet 2.3b: *Blank web of consequences*

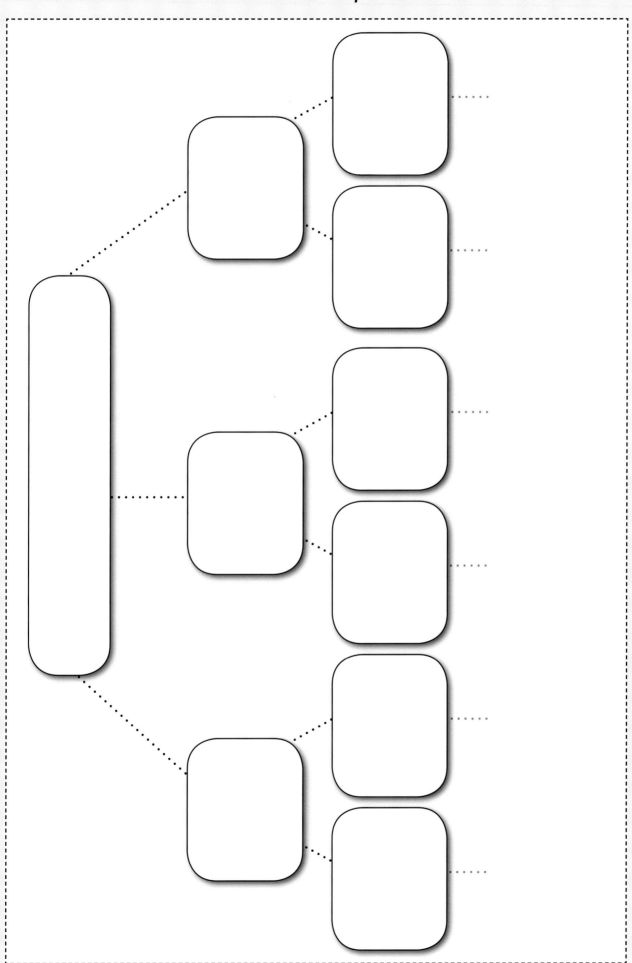

3 Changing bodies

In this lesson, pupils will explore the physical and emotional changes that take place during puberty. This lesson helps to equip children to understand strong feelings and emotions.

If possible, we recommend splitting up boys and girls into two single-sex classes for this lesson. This lesson may complement the Channel 4 *Sex and Relationship* DVD well.

Learning Objectives
• To reflect on the physical and emotional changes which take place during puberty.

Learning Outcomes
• I can describe how I will physically and emotionally change during puberty.

Lesson Activities and Resources
• Introduction: Changing bodies (15 minutes)
    Worksheet 3.1: *Changing bodies*
• Changing emotions (15 minutes)
    Worksheet 3.2: *Funny feelings*
• Plenary (15 minutes)

PSHE Curriculum
This lesson covers:
1.d. Pupils should be taught to recognise, as they approach puberty, how people's emotions change at that time and how to deal with their feelings towards themselves, their family and others in a positive way.
2.1. Pupils should be taught to appreciate the range of [national, regional] religions and [ethnic] identities in the United Kingdom
3.c. Pupils should be taught about how the body changes as they approach puberty.
5.i. During the key stage, pupils should be taught the knowledge, skills and understanding through opportunities to prepare for change.

Introduction - Changing bodies
25 minutes - Small group/whole class activity

Preparation: Each small group will need a copy of worksheet 3.1: *Changing bodies*. You will also need to project it onto the board later in the lesson.

- Write a definition of puberty on the board, e.g. 'the changes that take place in your body so you are able to make babies.'
- Explain that, during puberty, your body changes physically and you change psychologically to prepare you for having children.
- Divide the class into small groups and give each group a copy of worksheet 3.1: *Changing bodies.*
- Give pupils a few minutes to label the bodies with as many physical changes as they can think of that take place during puberty. Changes that happen to both girls and boys should be put between the two figures with arrows to both. You may want to emphasise that, within reason, any language they know to explain these changes can be used – they do not have to use 'technical terms'.
- After a minute, ask each group to pass their worksheet one group to the left so they can check each other's work.
- Go round the class asking each group to read out one change and add these to the worksheet 3.1: *Changing bodies,* projected on the board. The group with the most correct changes wins.
- Use the list of changes below to mark on any additional things that the class have missed off. Possible questions for discussion include:
  - Are there any words you do not understand?
  - Do any of these things surprise you?
  - How do you think it feels to have a body that seems to be changing all the time?
  - Does the idea of becoming an adult make you feel excited or scared?

Both sexes	Women	Men
• Pubic hair under arms and around groin/bottom	• Breasts grow	• Voice breaking
• Thicker, darker hair on legs	• Hips widen	• Wet dreams
• Body odour	• Waist becomes more narrow	• Facial hair
• Growing taller	• Periods start	• Thicker, darker hair on arms and chest
• Acne/greasier skin	• Discharge from vagina	• Shoulders broaden out
• Fatigue		• Spontaneous erections
• Growing pains		• Muscles grow
		• Some men will develop a small amount of breast tissue during puberty, but this usually disappears by the age of 20

Changing emotions
30 minutes - Pairs activity

Preparation: Each pair will need a copy of worksheet 3.2: *Funny feelings.*

- Using the emoticons on the worksheet for inspiration, pupils should then write or draw the emotions they think the person would feel in the box next to the statement.
- Whole class discussion using the following questions:
  - How do you think Jack and Mollie feel in these situations?
  - How do you think these new emotions might affect the way they behave?
  - Do you think that they have control over how they feel and act?
  - 'Teenagers often feel angry without knowing why': what could you do to help yourself understand your feelings better? To whom might you talk?

Extension questions

- Can you think of another embarrassing or confusing situation Jack or Mollie might experience as they go through puberty?
- Think about your own life. Are there times when you have felt embarrassed or shy about your body? What do you think would have made you feel less embarrassed?

Plenary
15 minutes - Pairs activity

- Choose one of the situations from worksheet 3.2: *Funny feelings.* What advice would you give to Jack or Mollie in this situation? How could they make the situation better?
- Feedback a few pairs' suggestions to the class.

There is an optional activity on masturbation on page 65 for those schools wishing to discuss this topic in the Changing bodies lesson.

Worksheet 3.1: *Changing bodies*

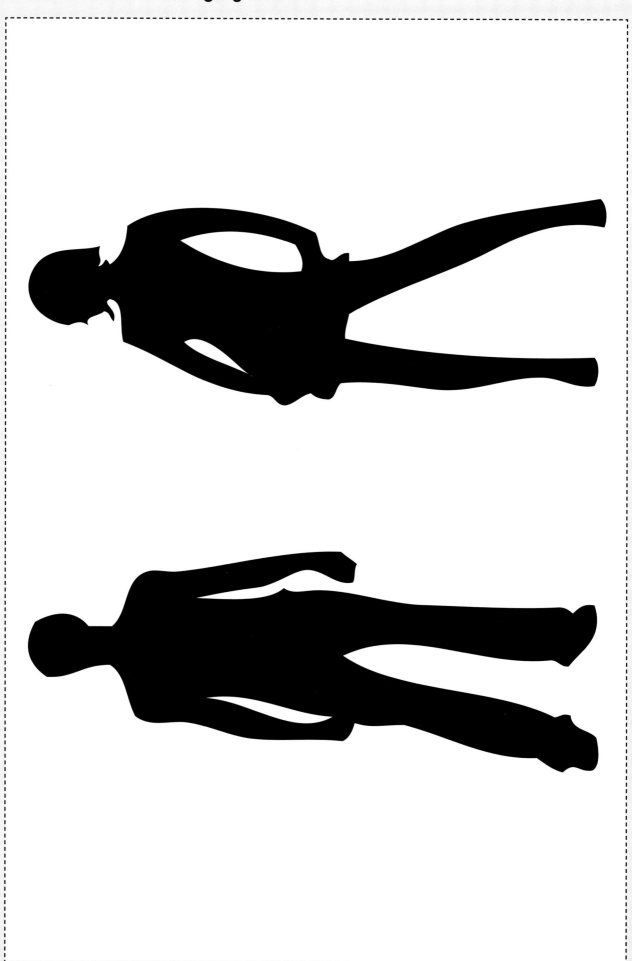

Worksheet 3.2: *Funny feelings*

Confused?   Frustrated?   Alone?   In love?   Happy?   Embarrassed?   Proud?

Angry?   Upset?   Annoyed?   Popular?   Grown up?   Not grown up?   Nervous?

Use the emotions and emoticons above to fill in the table below.
Draw or write at least three in each box.
Can you think of any other feelings Mollie and Jack might have?
Write these in the boxes as well.

Situation	How would Mollie or Jack feel?
Mollie has swimming on Tuesdays, but she has just started her period so cannot go this week. None of her friends have their periods yet.	
Jack has started to get acne, so his mum keeps telling him he needs to wash more.	
Jack's parents said he is not allowed to stay at his friend's party past 10pm, even though all his friends plan to stay past midnight.	
Mollie's best friend has invited her to the cinema and the boy she fancies is going. Mollie's mum wants to come with her, because she thinks she is too young to go on her own.	
Mollie has to wear a bra for the first time.	

Firm foundations

In this lesson, pupils will consider what character traits would help build strong foundations for a long-lasting relationship. They will reflect on what things are important in deciding whom to date, considering how necessary shared interests are, as well as what characteristics are important. Pupils will also consider the advantages and disadvantages of remaining single and in what ways this can be a positive life choice. The aim of this lesson is to equip pupils to be able to make well-considered decisions about whom they date.

Learning Objectives
- To reflect on how you choose your friends or a partner i.e. what things it is important to have in common/not in common.
- To consider what characteristics will help build strong foundations for a relationship.

Learning Outcomes
- I can describe characteristics that will help build a good relationship and why these are important.
- I can explain what sort of things I might look for in a friend or a partner and why.

Lesson Activities and Resources
- Introduction: Crazy characteristics (10 minutes)
- Dolly mixing (30 minutes)
> Worksheet 4.1: *Dolly profile*
> Worksheet 4.2: *Dolly feedback*
- Plenary: Another perspective (10 minutes)

PSHE Curriculum
This lesson covers:
1.a. Pupils should be taught to recognise their worth as individuals by identifying positive things about themselves and their achievements, seeing their mistakes, making amends and setting personal goals.
4.c. Pupils should be taught to be aware of different types of relationship, including marriage and those between friends and families, and to develop the skills to be effective in relationships.

Introduction - Crazy characteristics
10 minutes - Whole class activity

- Draw the outline of a person on the board.
- Ask pupils to suggest characteristics that would guarantee that no one ever wanted to go out with you! Write these around the person.
- Read out the following statement and ask pupils to do thumbs up/thumbs down to show whether or not they agree:

  'There is no point dating someone if you know you would not want to marry them.'

- Ask a few pupils to explain why they hold their opinion.

Dolly mixing
30 minutes - Small group activity

The aim of this activity is to think about compatibility (i.e. what makes two people 'compatible'); if necessary/more appropriate, it can be done in the context of an arranged marriage. It is also possible that some pupils may bring up the topic of homosexuality. Teachers can refer children back to their parents and explain that this subject will be dealt with in more detail in Key Stage 4.

Preparation: Each small group will need a copy of worksheet 4.1: *Dolly profile* and a copy of worksheet 4.2: *Dolly feedback*.

Part 1
10 minutes

- Put pupils into small groups of around three or four, so that you have an even number of groups.
- Give each group a copy of worksheet 4.1: *Dolly profile*; this will be the basis for their group's 'dolly'.
- The group should choose whether their character is 'male' or 'female'; they should give it a name and decide what it looks like, drawing features on to the dolly on the worksheet. They should then circle three words in each of the top three columns, and one word from each of the bottom three columns to define their dolly's personality.
- Once they have done this, give each dolly a number (e.g. F1, F2 etc. for female and M1, M2 etc. for males) to help discussion later on.

Part 2
20 minutes

- Each group is now going to take their character 'dolly mixing'.
- Give each group worksheet 4.2: *Dolly feedback,* on which they should write down whether they think the characters they meet would be compatible with theirs and why.
- Allocate a number of tables around the room as 'mixing points'.
- Half the groups will remain stationary; these groups should stand behind a table, facing into the room.
- The other groups will be mobile, moving from one table to the next. They should all start standing in front of a table, facing a stationary group.
- The groups have two minutes in which to find out as much as they can about the other person and decide how compatible their dolls would be.
- After two minutes, the inner (mobile) groups should move a table to the left and repeat the process. It does not matter if not every group meets every other group.
- Feedback to the class. Suggested questions for discussion include:
  - Of the dollies you met, who did you think would be the most compatible with your dolly and why?
  - What things do you think it is important for 'partners' to have in common? What does not matter? Why?
  - Do you think romance is a good way to choose a partner? Why/why not?

Extension question

- Write the following statement on the board and ask pupils whether or not they agree:

  'No one is perfect, so no relationship can be perfect. If you accept this, you will be happier.'

Plenary: Another perspective
20 minutes - Pairs/whole class activity

- Do you think there is someone for everyone or is it better for some people to stay single?
- Is being single a good life choice?
- In pairs, ask pupils to think of as many advantages and disadvantages to remaining single as they can. They should write these in two lists.
- Feedback, asking some pupils to read out their ideas. Write these up on the board.

Extension question

- Many religions think staying single is honourable because it allows you to focus on God. Why do you think you would be able to focus on God more? Is this a good reason to remain single?

Worksheet 4.1: *Dolly profile*

- Decide on a name for your 'dolly'.
- Draw in the physical appearance of your person on your 'dolly'.

Circle **THREE** statements from each column for your dolly

Likes	**Dislikes**	**Characteristics**
Racing cars	Racing cars	Happy
Computer games	Computer games	Sad
Board games	Board games	Angry
Shopping	Shopping	Sociable
Watching TV	Watching TV	Patient
Playing cards	Playing cards	Kind
Reading	Reading	Generous
Cats	Cats	Excitable
Dogs	Dogs	Energetic
Football	Football	Grumpy
Table football	Table football	Laid back
Basketball	Basketball	Fun
Tennis	Tennis	Boring
Rugby	Rugby	Nervous
Beach volleyball	Beach volleyball	Shy
Snooker	Snooker	Hard-working
Pool	Pool	Anti-social
Pop music	Pop music	
Indie music	Indie music	
Hip Hop music	Hip Hop music	
R 'n' B music	R 'n' B music	
Rock music	Rock music	
Science	Science	
Maths	Maths	
English	English	
Art	Art	
Gardening	Gardening	
Cinema	Cinema	

Choose ONE statement from each column for your dolly.

Beliefs	**Habits**	**Value statements**
Spiritual but not religious	Loves cleaning all the time	God gives me the power to love others
Christian	Is very messy	Everyone for themselves
Humanist (no God – humans the highest power)	Picks his/her nose	Success is all that matters
Buddhist	Scratches his/her bottom	We must build community
Hindu	Leaves the cap off the toothpaste	I treat others as I would like to be treated myself
Muslim	Leaves hair in the plughole	We must save the planet
Jewish	Puts everything in order	Animals have as much value as humans
Sikh	Bites his/her nails	
	Says 'you know' at the end of every sentence	

Worksheet 4.1: *Dolly profile (cont)*

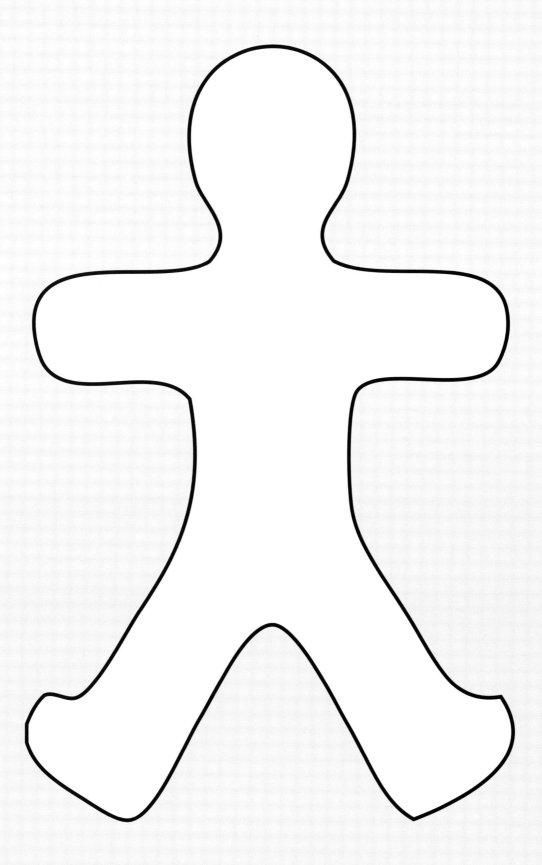

Worksheet 4.2: *Dolly feedback*

Write down the things you like and the things you dislike about each dolly you meet.

Doll	Name	Notes	Friend	More	Order of attraction
M1					
M2					
M3					
M4					
F1					
F2					
F3					
F4					

 Marriage

In this lesson, pupils will reflect on the significance and meaning of the wedding service and marriage. They will use the marriage vows from the Church of England marriage service to reflect on the magnitude of marriage. They will also consider the role of marriage in developing character and spirituality, as well as the benefits of marriage for the wider community/society. Pupils will be encouraged to understand why the institution of marriage is still widely respected and upheld, in spite of the secularisation of society.

This lesson could be taught in the context of a visit to a local church. The vicar may be able to help pupils stage a mock wedding.

Alternatively, you could invite a married couple from a local church to talk about what their wedding meant to them, what they enjoy about being married and how they sustain their marriage when life is hard.

Learning Objectives
- Reflect on the significance and meaning of an Anglican wedding service and marriage.
- Think about how marriage provides a strong foundation for relationships inside the family and with the wider community.

Learning Outcomes
- I can describe why Christians think marriage is important.
- I can explain how marriage is good for relationships within the family and with the wider community.

Lesson Activities and Resources
- Introduction: Mock wedding (15 minutes)
    - Powerpoint/worksheet 5.1: *Declaration and vows from the Marriage Service*
- Marriage vows (15 minutes)
    - Powerpoint/worksheet 5.2: *Promises*
- To marry or not to marry? (20 minutes)
    - Worksheet 5.3: *Why marry?*
- Plenary: Reflection (10 minutes)

PSHE Curriculum
This lesson covers:
2.e. to reflect on spiritual, moral, social, and cultural issues, using imagination to understand other people's experiences.
4.c. to be aware of different types of relationship, including marriage and those between friends and families, and to develop the skills to be effective in relationships.

Introduction - Mock wedding
15 minutes - Whole class activity

Preparation: If holding the mock wedding away from the classroom, then print copies of worksheet 5.1: *Declaration and vows from the Marriage Service* instead of using it projected onto the board.

- Use the Declaration and Vows from the Church of England marriage service to help pupils stage a mock wedding. You will need:
  - A groom
  - A bride
  - The vicar (this part has significantly more words, so it is suitable for a very able pupil, or possibly a teacher)
  - Congregation (rest of class)
- Project the Declaration and Vows onto the board and act out this part of the ceremony.
- Discussion:
  - What else happens during a wedding?
  - What do you think is the most important part of the wedding? Why?

Marriage vows
15 minutes - Small group activity

This activity gives pupils the opportunity to explore two of the marriage vows in more detail. (For more able pupils, you may wish to pick a third vow: 'for better, for worse', or 'to love and to cherish until death us do part'.)

Preparation: Each small group will need a copy of worksheet 5.2: *Promises.* Alternatively you can project the powerpoint version onto the board.

- Give each small group a copy of worksheet 5.2: *Promises.*
- In groups, ask pupils to fill in the table, explaining why each vow is important and describing a situation when it might be hard to keep this promise.
- Feedback to the whole class.

Extension questions

- Write the following statement on the board:
  'Having a big public wedding means you will stay married forever.'
- Do you agree?
- What is more important: the wedding day or the marriage?

To marry or not to marry?

20 minutes - Small group activity

Preparation: Each small group will need one copy of worksheet 5.3: *Why marry?* To save time you may want to cut out the nine diamond cards beforehand.

- Give out a set of cards from worksheet 5.3: *Why marry?* to each group. Explain that every card has on it a potential benefit of marriage, which might motivate someone to choose to get married over not getting married.
- Ask pupils to arrange these in the shape of a diamond (1 – 2 – 3 – 2 – 1), with the reasons that they think are the best/most important at the top, and the reasons they think are least important/bad at the bottom.
- Feedback to the class, starting discussion with the following questions:
  - Which reasons did you think were good/bad? Why?
  - Why do some people choose not to marry?
  - Given all the possible benefits of marriage on the cards, why do you think some marriages don't last?

Plenary: Reflection

10 minutes - Whole class activity

- Put the following statement on the board:
  'Christians believe that God joins people together and promises to be with them on their journey, so marriages where people believe in God are more likely to last.'
- Mark one side of the room as 'agree' and the other as 'disagree'.
- Ask pupils to move to the side of the room that shows their opinion of this statement.
- Ask a few pupils to explain why they hold this opinion.
  - Did any of the opinions you heard today give you a new perspective on marriage?

Worksheet 5.1: *Declaration and vows from the Marriage Service*

The Declarations

The minister says to the congregation
First, I am required to ask anyone present who knows a reason why these persons
may not lawfully marry, to declare it now.

The minister says to the couple
The vows you are about to take are to be made in the presence of God,
who is judge of all and knows all the secrets of our hearts; therefore if either of you
knows a reason why you may not lawfully marry, you must declare it now.

The minister says to the bridegroom
N, will you take N to be your wife?
Will you love her, comfort her, honour and protect her, and, forsaking all others,
be faithful to her as long as you both shall live?

He answers   **I will.**

The minister says to the bride
N, will you take N to be your husband?
Will you love him, comfort him, honour and protect him, and, forsaking all others,
be faithful to him as long as you both shall live?

She answers   **I will.**

The minister says to the congregation
Will you, the families and friends of N and N, support and uphold them in their
marriage now and in the years to come?

All   **We will.**

The Vows

The minister introduces the vows in these or similar words
N and N, I now invite you to join hands and make your vows, in the presence
of God and his people.

The bride and bridegroom face each other.
The bridegroom takes the bride's right hand in his.

These words are used
I, N , take you, N , to be my wife, to have and to hold from this day forward;
for better, for worse, for richer, for poorer, in sickness and in health, to love
and to cherish, till death us do part; according to God's holy law. In the presence
of God I make this vow.

They loose hands.
The bride takes the bridegroom's right hand in hers, and says
I, N , take you, N , to be my husband, to have and to hold from this day forward;
for better, for worse, for richer, for poorer, in sickness and in health, to love and
to cherish, till death us do part; according to God's holy law. In the presence
of God I make this vow.

Worksheet 5.2: *Promises*

Vow	Why is this an important promise to make if you want your marriage to last?	Describe a situation when it might be hard to keep this promise.
In sickness and in health		
For richer, for poorer		

Worksheet 5.3: *Why marry?*

We have made a
new family together and
become part of each
other's families.

Being married means
we have a stable home
to bring up our
children in.

I enjoy being loved
and having someone else
to love. I feel safe because
we have promised to
stay together.

We can learn
about God together.

Being married
helps us learn to be less
selfish and not always
expect to have our
own way.

We share everything,
including our money
and special belongings.

I get to share the
washing up and cleaning.

I can live with
my best friend and get
to know them better
throughout
our life together.

We help one another
become the best people
we can be.
We can be completely
honest with each other.

Lesson 6 Great expectations?

In this lesson, pupils will discuss the advantages of keeping sex for marriage/ long-term relationships. They will reflect on what their expectations for sex are and from where these ideas might have come. They will consider Christian and other world faith perspectives on the meaning and significance of sex and be encouraged to think about the benefits of saving sex for long-term, committed relationships.

This lesson assumes that students understand what conception is and how it occurs. Teachers may choose to cover this by using materials such as the Channel 4 series *Living and Growing*; the Christopher Winter Project Year 6 lesson 3 *Conception and Pregnancy*; or materials from *In the Beginning* from St. Edward's RC School, Lees Oldham.

Learning Objectives
- Consider the significance of sex within different cultural and religious contexts and understand why these opinions are held.
- Discuss why it is often considered best to keep sex for marriage/long-term relationships.

Learning Outcomes
- I can explain what I think 'healthy sexual behaviour' is and why I think this.
- I can describe what some religions and cultures think about sex.
- I can give reasons why it might be good for sex to be kept for a marriage or long-term relationship.

Lesson Activities and Resources
- Introduction: Talking about sex (5 minutes)
  - Sex is for... (20 minutes)
  - Worksheet 6.1: *Sex is for...*
- Great expectations? (25 minutes)
  - Worksheet 6.2a/6.2b: *Great expectations?*
  - Worksheet 6.3: *Who thinks...?*
  - Powerpoint 6.4: *How sex affects a person*
- Plenary: I think sex is... (10 minutes)

PSHE Curriculum
This lesson covers:
2.e. Pupils should be taught to reflect on spiritual, moral, social, and cultural issues, using imagination to understand other people's experiences.
4.b. Pupils should be taught to think about the lives of people living in other places and times, and people with different values and customs.

Introduction - Talking about sex
5 minutes - Whole class activity

- Listen to an contemporary song about relationships, and if appropriate show the music video e.g. Taylor Swift, 'Love Story' (*Fearless*, 2008); or a classic pop song e.g. The Beatles, 'When I'm 64' (*Sgt. Pepper's Lonely Hearts Club Band*, 1967).

Sex is for...
20 minutes - Small group activity

Preparation: Each small group will need both pages of worksheet 6.1: *Sex is for...*

- Ask pupils to cut out the statements for the 'What is sex for?' section of worksheet 6.1: *Sex is for...* adding their own ideas into the blank cards if they want, then sort them into the 'true' and 'false' columns (if necessary, add a 'not sure' column).
- They should then do the same thing for the 'Who is sex for?' section.
- Feedback to the group:
  - Which statements do pupils agree/disagree with?
  - Which perspectives or ideas are new to them?

Extension question

- As a group, make up your own statement summarising what you think sex is for.

Great expectations?
25 minutes - Small group activity

Preparation: There are two versions of the *Great expectations?* worksheet, 6.2a and 6.2b. Worksheet 6.2b is simpler and so may be more appropriate for some classes. Each small group will need a copy of worksheet 6.2a/6.2b: *Great expectations?* and a copy of worksheet 6.3: *Who thinks...?*

Part 1

- Explain that people have different opinions on when you can have sex. This is because of different cultural traditions, different religious beliefs and different personal perspectives. However, most people in the world believe that sex is best as part of a long-term committed relationship or marriage. This is because sex is a very intimate act.
- Give each small group a copy of 6.2a/6.2b: *Great expectations* and a copy of worksheet 6.3: *Who thinks...?*

- Pupils should fill in worksheet 6.3: *Who thinks...?*, using the opinions on worksheet 6.2a/6.2b: *Great expectations?*
- Feedback to the class and discussion:
  - What are the reasons these people have decided to wait/not to wait?
  - Do you think they have good reasons for their choices?

Part 2

Depending on group dynamics, this could also be done as a whole class activity.

Preparation: Each small group will need a copy of worksheet 6.2a/6.2b: *Great expectations?* as used in Part 1.

- Project powerpoint/worksheet 6.4: *How does sex affect a person* onto the board.
- In small groups, ask pupils to use the ideas bank and the opinions on worksheet 6.2a/6.2b: *Great expectations?* to identify the ways that having sex might affect a person emotionally, spiritually and physically. Some ideas may go in more than one place.
- Encourage pupils to come up with their own ideas as well.
- After a discussion in groups, feedback to class, adding possible effects to the diagram on the board.
  - Are there any ideas that pupils do not understand?

Note to teachers

In Christianity, sex is understood to bring people closer to God for a number of reasons. Two people becoming one with each other is seen to echo the close relationship between God and humanity, where God's love is so secure that complete vulnerability and openness is possible. The intimacy of sex teaches people to give and receive, as well as to love more profoundly. As we develop such characteristics as these, we become more like God intended us to be, and so draw closer to him. Christians also believe that God wants to bless people in all things and that includes the intimacy of sexual union.

Plenary: I think sex is...
10 minutes - Whole class activity

- Discussion, using the following questions:
  - If having sex can affect people in all these different ways, when might it be a good time for them to start having sex?
  - Which out of the emotional, physical and spiritual effects listed do you think might have the biggest impact on a person's life? Why?

Worksheet 6.1: *Sex is for...*

What is sex for?

Making children	**Feeling loved**
Growing closer to someone emotionally	**Showing someone you love them**
Growing closer to someone spiritually	**Having fun**
Growing closer to God	**Making me happy**
Showing someone you are committed to them	**Making the other person happy**

Who is sex for?

Someone special	**Children**
Anyone	**Married people**
Grown ups	**Unmarried people**
Teenagers	

Worksheet 6.1: *Sex is for... (cont)*

What is sex for?

True	False

Who is sex for?

True	False

Worksheet 6.2a: *Great expectations?*

Ameena (Muslim)

I come from Pakistan and in my country you only have sex once you are married. This is because my country is Muslim and we believe that sex is an act of worship which brings you closer to God, and which is meant for a man and wife only.

Chloë (Atheist – Humanist – does not believe in a God)

I do not believe in God, but I do believe you should try to treat all people well. I think it is a bad idea to have sex with someone if you are not equally committed to each other, because one of you will probably get emotionally hurt. I also think it would be weird to share something so personal with someone you didn't love.

Marie (Christian – Church of England)

Marriage is a spiritual way of life, a joining together of two people by God. Sex is a physical expression of this joining together which brings you very close to the other person. I think God made sex for marriage, so it is best to keep it this way.

Giovanni (Christian – Catholic)

I believe that having children is a really important part of sex. I think that it is best to bring children up in a family so having sex before you are married is a bad idea. I also believe that sex is a gift from God, which he intended for marriage. If I live the way God wants me to, I believe that I will be a fuller person.

Krishna (Hindu)

I have been brought up with very strict rules about sex. Our faith states that it is important to be self-controlled and focus on learning about God. So before I am married I will not have close relationships with people of the other sex. When I am married I will have sex because it will make my relationship with my partner stronger.

Ruth (Jewish)

Within Judaism, marriage is seen as an extremely important physical (sex) and spiritual (love) relationship. Having children is part of that relationship. It is a response to G-d's commandment to 'be fruitful and multiply'.

Fred (Agnostic – unsure whether there is a God)

I believe the point of life is to be happy and help other people be happy. If having lots of sex makes you and the people you sleep with happy, then that's fine. But you should not take advantage of people or treat them in a way that makes them unhappy.

Joanna (Christian – Church of England)

I believe that God has given sex as a special gift that is best kept for marriage. However, I realise that I may find it hard to stick to that. A long-term relationship may be a bit like a marriage. I know God will always love me and wants a relationship with me throughout my life whatever I do.

Jasminder (Sikh)

Sikhs are forbidden to have sex before they are married. Once married, sex is less important than helping one another along the spiritual path. Not having sex for a period of time can help this. However, every couple should aim to contribute to Waheguru's (the one God) creation by having a family.

Worksheet from Love & Sex Matters, KS2 resources © Salisbury Diocesan Board of Education, Bristol Diocesan Board of Education & Hope's Place.

Worksheet 6.2b: *Great expectations? (version 2)*

Ameena (Muslim)
Sex is an act of worship which brings you closer to God. It is meant for a husband and a wife only.

Chloë (Atheist – Humanist – does not believe in a God)
I think you should try to treat all people well, so you should only have sex with someone if you are equally committed to each other.

Marie (Christian – Church of England)
Marriage is a spiritual joining together of two people by God. Sex is a way of showing this.

Giovanni (Christian – Catholic)
Having children is an important part of sex. The best time to have children is when you are married, so you should save sex for marriage.

Krishna (Hindu)
Self-control is very important. Before I am married I will not have close relationships with people of the other sex. I will have sex when I am married because sex makes a marriage stronger.

Ruth (Jewish)
Marriage brings physical (sex) and spiritual (love) fulfilment. Having children is an important part of sex and marriage. It is a commandment from G-d.

Fred (Agnostic – unsure whether there is a God)
The point of life is to be happy. It is fine to have lots of sex if it makes you happy, as long as your actions don't make other people sad.

Joanna (Christian – Church of England)
I think sex is best kept for marriage. I may find it hard to wait until I am married, and a long-term relationship may be a bit like a marriage. I know God will always love me throughout my life.

Jasminder (Sikh)
Sex before marriage is forbidden. Once married, continuing on the spiritual path is more important than having sex. However, every couple should aim to have a family one day.

Worksheet 6.3: *Who thinks...?*

Use worksheet 6.2: *Great expectations?* to help you fill in the grid below.
With which opinions do you agree?

	I would have sex before marriage	I would not have sex before marriage	Reason for my decision
Fred (Agnostic)			
Ruth (Jew)			
Krishna (Hindu)			
Giovanni (Christian – Catholic)			
Marie (Christian)			
Chloê (Atheist)			
Ameena (Muslim)			
Joanna (Christian – Church of England)			
Jasminder (Sikh)			

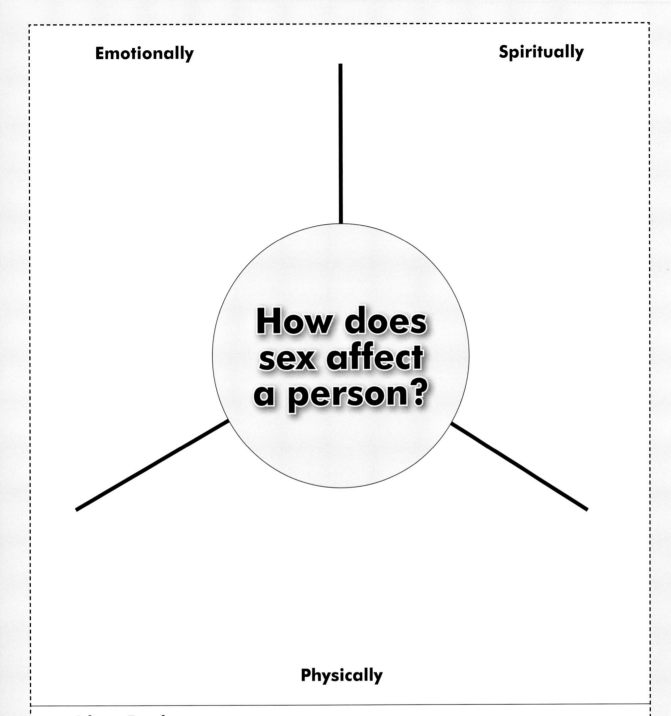

Emotionally

Spiritually

How does sex affect a person?

Physically

Ideas Bank:

- See someone else's body up close
- Feel loved
- Brought closer to God
- Could get a sexually transmitted infection, like HIV
- Share myself with someone else
- Joined with another person
- Feel attractive
- Feel more dependent on another person
- Learn more about another person

- Will feel more sad if the person breaks up with me

Lesson 7 In need of restoration?

In this lesson pupils will discuss the concept of forgiveness and the part it plays, or can play, in relationships. Pupils will engage in a practical activity using pebbles as a metaphor for how guilt and anger can build up and become a burden. Hypothetical scenarios will be used as a basis for discussing how and when forgiveness can be practised in relationships.

Learning Objectives
- Discuss when forgiveness can or should be shown.
- Reflect on how forgiveness benefits those who show and receive it.

Learning Outcomes
- I can explain why it is good to forgive people.
- I can describe some situations when I think you should or should not show forgiveness and explain why.

Lesson Activities and Resources
- Introduction: Forgiving words (5 minutes)
  - Building up baggage (40 minutes)
  - Worksheet 7.1: *Building up baggage*
  - Pebbles or similar
  - Three receptacles (bucket, bowl, shoe box etc)
- Plenary: Conscience alley (15 minutes)
  - Worksheet 7.2: *Conscience alley*
- Extension activity: To forgive or not to forgive? (20 minutes)
  - Worksheet 7.3: *To forgive or not to forgive?*

PSHE Curriculum
This lesson covers:

1.a. Pupils should be taught to talk and write about their opinions, and explain their views, on issues that affect themselves and society.

2.e. Pupils should be taught to reflect on spiritual, moral, social, and cultural issues, using imagination to understand other people's experiences.

5.g. Pupils should be taught the knowledge, skills and understanding through opportunities to consider social and moral dilemmas that they come across in life.

Introduction - Forgiving words
5 minutes - Whole class activity

- Write the following three words and their definitions on the board:
  Guilt: feeling bad about something you have done.
  Anger: feeling very cross or frustrated about something or with somebody.
  Forgiveness: being able to let go of something bad done to you; giving someone a fresh start.
- Ask pupils to construct some sentences using these words to show that they have understood them.

Building up baggage
40 minutes - Small group/whole class activity

Preparation: There are seven scenarios on worksheet 7.1: *Building up baggage*. Each small group should have a different scenario. Label one of the three receptacles 'Paige', one 'Laksh', and leave the third blank. Put pebbles in the blank one.

Part 1
10 minutes

- Divide the class into small groups and give each one a scenario from worksheet 7.1: *Building up baggage*. Explain that all the scenarios are about the same married couple.
- Ask each group to read their scenario and then discuss the following questions:
  - Who might be angry? Who might feel guilty?
  - What situation has made the person angry/guilty?

Part 2
15 minutes

- Put the three receptacles on the teacher's desk.
- Explain that the pebbles represent guilt and anger and the receptacles represent Paige and Laksh.
- Ask one group at a time to come up and present their situation to the class.
- After a group has explained their situation, ask them to conclude by completing the sentences: 'Laksh feels angry/guilty because...' and put a pebble in his receptacle; and 'Paige feels guilty/angry because...' and give her receptacle a pebble.
- Once all the groups have come up, ask two pupils to come up and demonstrate how heavy the receptacles are.

- Discuss what has happened; possible questions include:
  - How do the [receptacles] feel now? Why?
  - If the stones represent guilt and anger, how do guilt and anger affect Laksh and Paige?
  - How might this guilt and anger affect their relationship?

Part 3
15 minutes

- Give each group two minutes to try and work out possible solutions to their scenario:
  - What could make Paige/Laksh feel less angry?
  - What might help Paige/Laksh feel less guilty?
- After two minutes, invite each group back up to explain how their situation could be improved. This could be done as a semi-staged dialogue showing a conversation that Paige and Laksh might have in an attempt to resolve the tension.
- Once a group has done this, ask them to remove a pebble from Paige's and Laksh's receptacles if they think the situation has improved. If they do not think the situation can be changed, then they should not remove a pebble.
- Finally, demonstrate that the receptacles are lighter/empty. Follow with discussion of what has happened; possible questions include:
  - Do you think that Paige and Laksh mean to hurt each other?
  - How do you think it might affect the 'angry' person if he/she does not forgive someone?
  - How do you think it might affect the guilty person to know he/she has been forgiven?
  - Given that people frequently make mistakes, do you think that forgiveness is a one-off act or an on-going choice?

Extension questions

- Does forgiving someone mean pretending an event never happened?
- Some actions have permanent, negative consequences – do you think such actions would be harder to forgive?

Plenary - Conscience alley
15 minutes - Whole class activity

Preparation: Select two of the scenarios from worksheet 7.2: *Conscience alley.*

- Explain that in this activity pupils will think about whether everything is forgiveable and whether it is sometimes OK not to forgive.
- Divide the class into two equal-sized groups.

- Ask one pupil from each group to volunteer to be a character in a scenario, and give them the scenario to read.
- Within each group, ask the remaining pupils to form two lines that face each other, making an 'alley' for each character.
- The scenario character should read out the situation to his/her group and then begin to walk slowly down the alley.
- As the character walks along, each person in the line must say one sentence (out loud) explaining why they think the character should or should not forgive the person who has wronged him/her.
- Once each character has reached the end of the line, bring the whole class back together.
- Ask both characters to explain briefly their situation and then whether or not they want to forgive the people who have hurt them. Ask them to explain what has influenced this decision.
- Ask the class for their response:
  - How many of the group agree with their decisions? How many do not?
  - Why/why not?
  - Do you think that some things are 'unforgiveable'?

Extension activity - To forgive or not to forgive?
20 minutes - Small group activity

This activity can be used to extend the discussion on whether everything is forgiveable.

Preparation: Each small group will need six of the eight scenario cards from worksheet 7.3: *To forgive or not to forgive.* You may want to select those most appropriate for your class.

- Give each small group the six chosen scenario cards. Ask them to discuss each scenario, then put it into one of two piles: 'Forgiveable' and 'Unforgiveable'.
- When all the cards have been placed, initiate feedback to the class and discussion using the following questions:
  - Did everyone agree about which pile the cards should go in? Why/why not?
  - Can you just forgive someone, or should they be punished first?
  - 'Whether to forgive is a moral question – one should. Being able to forgive, on the other hand, is a spiritual question. As a human you can't do it alone; it is only possible with God's help.' Do you agree? Do you think forgiving is an easy thing to do?

Note to teachers

A good theological introduction to the concept of forgiveness is provided on the website www.christianvalues4schools.co.uk.

Worksheet 7.1: *Building up baggage*

Scenario 1
Paige has an important event at work this evening and Laksh is invited as well. But Laksh has forgotten that they were going out. He has gone to the pub with his friends on the way home from work. Paige will have to go without him.

Scenario 2
Paige is a really untidy person, which has always annoyed Laksh. When Laksh's grandparents ring to tell him that they are coming on a visit from India, he asks them to come round for a meal. Paige promises she will tidy up downstairs.
Laksh's grandparents are arriving in an hour. The house is still a complete tip. Paige has just left because she has arranged to meet friends. Laksh will have to tidy up the house on his own.

Scenario 3
Laksh had promised to take Paige out to the cinema as a treat on her birthday because she loves films. A few days before her birthday, Laksh's new boss asked him to attend a drinks party on the same day. It is really important for Laksh to go because he is working for a promotion. He tells Paige that her birthday celebration will have to wait.

Scenario 4
Laksh wants to have a quiet night in on Sunday. They have had people round almost every night that week and he is exhausted! Paige does not realise how tired Laksh is, and she invites some friends round. She doesn't tell Laksh her plans. Half an hour before their friends arrive, Paige mentions to Laksh that four friends are coming for dinner.

Scenario 5
Paige has wanted a new car for a long time. She and Laksh had worked out that if they saved up for a few months, she could get the car she had always dreamed of. They had saved up almost enough money when Laksh comes home one day with a very expensive new guitar. He has spent a large chunk of her car money without thinking it through.

Scenario 6
Christmas is important to Laksh. His father died on Christmas Day, so his close family always get together to remember him. Paige was worried her mother would be upset if she missed the family Christmas gathering. She told her mum that she and Laksh would be at the family gathering, without asking Laksh. One evening, Laksh asks if they can talk about where they are going for Christmas. Paige has to say that she has already decided for them.

Scenario 7
Paige wants to be a mum. Before Paige and Laksh got married they talked about children. Laksh said that he was really happy to have children and did not mind if Paige wanted to start their family soon. But when Paige says she would like to have a baby soon, Laksh tells her that he had been lying and he does not want children for a few more years.

Worksheet 7.2: *Conscience alley*

Scenario 1

One of the boys in my class spread a nasty rumour, saying that I kissed another girl.
Now everyone sniggers at me when I walk past and my friends are really awkward
around me.
Can/should I forgive him?

Scenario 2

My brother keeps on trashing my bedroom, throwing all my stuff round everywhere.
He says it's because I have babyish toys.
Can/should I forgive him?

Scenario 3

My mum said that I cannot go to my friend's party because it is inconvenient for her to
take me and she needs me to look after my little brother while she goes to a meeting.
Can/should I forgive her?

Scenario 4

My parents have decided that I have to move schools, even though I really don't want to.
Their only reason is that it is closer to home.
Can/should I forgive them?

Worksheet 7.3: *To forgive or not to forgive?*

1

My little sister stole all the sweets from the cupboard and lied to my mum, saying that I did it. I was the one who got told off.
Can/should I forgive her?

2

I am always scared walking home because a group of boys waits to beat me up. If they catch me, they take stuff from my school bag and hit me with it, until they get bored.
Can/should I forgive them?

3

My best friend has decided that the new person in our class is cooler than me, so he/she doesn't want to hang out with me any more.
Can/should I forgive him/her?

4

My brother's girlfriend cheated on him. She kissed another guy and now he is not sure whether he wants to go out with her any more.
Can/should he forgive her?

5

I read a story in the newspaper about some teenagers who killed a young boy in a racist attack.
Can/should they be forgiven?

6

My big brother had too much to drink last night and accidentally broke my dad's new computer.
Can/should he be forgiven?

7

My mum is always late picking me up from school because she is so busy at work. Yesterday she forgot altogether and I had to go home with someone else.
Can/should I forgive her?

8

My Dad promised he'd come to the school show because I was singing. The day before he said he had a work meeting that he just couldn't miss, so he couldn't come to the show.
Can/should I forgive him?

Summary activities

These activities aim to encourage pupils' spiritual development. They are designed to draw the course together, allowing pupils to reflect on what they have learnt and its application to their lives. These contemplative activities are centred around the following three questions:

- What makes a relationship good for those in it?
- What makes a relationship bad for those in it?
- How could I change so that my approach to relationships is more 'life-giving'?

Note to teachers
Teachers are reminded that relationships, particularly life-limiting relationships, may be a sensitive topic for some children, so activities should be undertaken with due care.

Card sorting
10 minutes - Small group activity

Preparation: Each small group will need a set of cards from worksheet 8.1: *Values for relationships action cards.*

- Write the following definitions on the board:
  'A life-giving relationship helps the people in it be the best they can be.'
  'A life-limiting relationship stops one or both of the people in it being the best they can be.'
- Give each small group the *Values for relationships action cards.*
  Explain that they show different actions or characteristics that a person might take/show in a relationship.
- Ask pupils to sort the cards into three columns headed:
  - Life-giving behaviour (i.e. 'help us be the best we can be')
  - Life-limiting behaviour (i.e. 'stops one or both of us being the best we can be')
  - Could be either (depending on the context).
- Ask groups to add their own ideas to the two blank cards.
- Feedback, using the following questions:
  - Which cards were the most difficult to place? Why?

- Pick a statement which could go in either column depending on the nature of the people involved e.g. 'wants to spend all his/her free time with me'. Look at it more carefully by asking pupils questions such as:
    - What would be good about having a friend who wanted to spend all his/her free time with you?
    - If you spent all your free time with one person, how might this affect the other relationships in your life?
    - How does the fact we are all different affect what we need in a relationship? Do you think there are some things that everyone needs?

Personal reflection
10 minutes - Individual activity

- Give each child a piece of paper and, if you like, put some background music on (suggestions for music below).
- Ask them to write about or draw a picture illustrating a time when they have treated someone in a life-giving way.
- Then, ask them to write about or draw a picture illustrating a time when they have treated someone in a life-limiting way.
- Ask each pupil to think of one way that they could be more life-giving in their relationships this week. They could write this aim in a prominent place (e.g. in the front of a workbook or homework diary) to remind them about it over the coming week.

Relevant music

Sydney Carter, 'When I needed a neighbour', available in many collections of worship songs.
Matt Redman, 'The Father's Song' on The Father's Song (Survivor, 2006)
Becky Frith – You'll Be There, album available online as a CD, or downloads, at www.beckyfrith.com

Worksheet 8.1: *Values for relationships action cards*

Relationships that bring people alive are life-giving; relationships that take advantage of people or break them down are life-limiting or abusive. The cards show different actions and characteristics. Sort them into two columns: life-giving, and life-limiting.

1 Listens to what I say	**2** Always lets me have my own way	**3** Always bosses me around	**4** Is kind
5 Is lazy and makes me do everything	**6** Gets angry if I disagree with him/her	**7** Likes to tell me who I can be friends with	**8** Encourages me to do things my parents are not happy about
9 Cares about what I think	**10** Is always miserable	**11** Wants to spend all his/her free time with me	**12** Looks after me when life is difficult
13 Lies to me	**14** Is always bouncy and cheerful	**15** Drinks too much alcohol	**16** Is selfish
17 Always thinks of others first	**18** Gives me space to be me	**19** Is mean	**20** Only talks about what he/she finds interesting
21 Always sees the best in me	**22** Is embarrassed to let me meet his/her other friends		

Optional Material

Changing bodies: Masturbation

Questions are sometimes raised at Key Stage 2 about the topic of masturbation. We have therefore provided some optional material on this subject that schools can choose to use, or adapt, if they decide it is appropriate for their pupils. This material could also be used with Key Stage 3 pupils and is included as optional material in the KS3 *Love and Sex Matters* resource.

Children and young teenagers will pick up messages about sex from many sources including the TV, music, the Internet, magazines, friends, home and school and this will naturally lead them to ask questions about sex and relationships, including possibly questions about masturbation. This activity gives them the opportunity to think about this topic in a safe context. These activities can provide pupils with an opportunity to discuss masturbation, as they reflect on Christian and other faith perspectives on this topic.

We recognise, however, that some schools and governing bodies may feel that masturbation is an unsuitable topic for Key Stage 2 and will choose to omit this section.

Learning Objectives
- To consider what Christianity and other world religions think about masturbation

---

Learning Outcomes
- I can explain what Christianity and other world religions think about masturbation and give my own opinion

---

Lesson Resources
- Worksheet 9.1: *Masturbation opinions*
- Worksheet 9.2: *Who thinks masturbation is...?*

Masturbation
20 minutes - Small group activity

Preparation: Each small group will need between six and nine different masturbation discussion cards from worksheet 9.1: *Masturbation opinions* (depending on students' age/ability). There are nine on the sheet. Each group will also need a copy of worksheet 9.2: *Who thinks masturbation is...?*

- Write a definition of masturbation on the board e.g. 'rubbing your genitals so that it feels nice'.
- Give each group cards from worksheet 9.1: *Masturbation opinions* and worksheet 9.2: *Who thinks masturbation is...?*
- Ask pupils to place each card at a point between the 'good' and 'bad' end of the line that reflects the opinion given.
- After pupils have placed all their cards, discuss what they have found.
  - Which opinion do you most agree with and why?

Plenary
10 minutes - Whole class activity

- Start class discussion with the following questions:
  - Why do you think people masturbate?
  - Can you suggest some times or places when/where it might be inappropriate to masturbate?
- Read out the following statement from the NHS website and ask pupils to do thumbs up/thumbs down to show whether or not they agree:
  'Masturbation can do you no emotional harm.'[10]
- Ask a few pupils to explain why they hold this opinion.

---

10. NHS, 'Is It normal To Masturbate? NHS [online], (15 January 2009). Available at http://www.nhs.ik/chq/Pages/1684.aspx?CategoryID= 118&SubCategoryID=122 [accessed 1 September 2009].

Worksheet 9.1: *Masturbation opinions*

Krishna (Hindu)
Masturbation takes up time that could be better used for spiritual things.
Besides, you should learn to control your sex drive and not have it control you.

Hari (Buddhist)
One of our five moral teachings says you should avoid 'sexual misconduct'.
So every Buddhist has to work out for themselves whether it is OK to masturbate.

Marie (Christian)
I believe God gave me sexual desires so God understands when I masturbate.
I think it would be wrong if it became obsessive or it stopped me living a full life
to God's glory.

Ameena (Muslim)
The Qu'ran says that 'those who guard their virginity are free from blame'.
I think that masturbation is only OK if you do it to stop yourself committing a sexual sin.

Jasminder (Sikh)
I believe lust is one of the five vices, which stop you from reaching perfection.
It is hard to masturbate without lusting after other people.

Giovanni (Christian)
I believe that God made sex as a sacred act to bring you closer to your husband or wife.
If you use it any other way it will be less fulfilling. Also, it is hard to masturbate without
fantasising about another person and it can become addictive, so I try not to.

Fred (Agnostic – unsure whether there is a God)
I think masturbating is a good way of helping control your sex drive when you are
growing up. It is definitely better than sleeping around.

Chloë (Atheist – does not believe in a God)
Although no one talks about it much, most of my friends masturbate. There aren't any
health risks, but my doctor did say you can become addicted, so I try not to do
it very often.

Ruth (Jewish)
As an Orthodox Jew, I have been taught that the Talmud says that you should not waste
sperm, because it is meant for creating babies, so I don't think men should masturbate.
I am aware that other Jews may have different opinions.

Worksheet from Love & Sex Matters, KS2 resources © Salisbury Diocesan Board of Education, Bristol Diocesan Board of Education & Hope's Place.

Worksheet 9.2: Who thinks masturbation is...?

BAD

GOOD

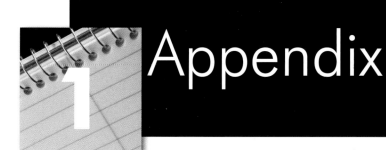

Appendix

Values related questions for pupils to explore throughout KS1 and KS2

Values are principles or convictions that act as a guide to behaviour. All schools promote a core set of values, which are shared and explored within the context of the school community. For church schools these shared values will naturally be rooted in the wisdom and understanding of the Christian faith and particularly in gospel values. As pupils explore, question and experience these values they are able to consider how Christian values are the same or different from the 21st-century values of a secular society. They are also provided with a safe environment where they can consider the ways in which a particular value might be applied in a range of situations, and also grapple with controversial issues. Whilst the values listed below have been chosen as being distinctively Christian we recognize that many of these values will also be shared with community schools and those of other faiths.

For each value a number of questions have been highlighted which relate specifically to relationships and sex education. Therefore, in order to support work undertaken in SRE, it is suggested that as each chosen value is explored within your school community these questions are also considered and reflected upon – e.g. in classroom activities; collective worship; in staff discussion and in discussions with key stakeholders. These questions will therefore be explored as a child progresses through the Primary phase in an age-appropriate way.

The values listed include those contained within the *Values for Life* resource used currently by many church primary schools; Shahne Vickery, Catherine Coster and Verity Holloway, *Values for Life* (Jumping Fish, Diocese of Gloucester).

Courage

Discuss times when you need to have courage to:
- Say no
- To share fears and worries
- Be yourself
- To ask questions
- To stand up for what is right.

Trust

- Who can I trust?
- Why should we be trustworthy?
- How do I maintain trust?
- What happens when trust is broken?

Consider aspects of:
- Being trustworthy
- Trusting in yourself.

Creativity

Explore the Christian belief that we are each unique and special – made in the image of God:
- Why am I unique and precious?
- How am I made in God's image?
- What am I here for?
- Who am I?
- Who made me?
- How is life a gift?
- How can I be a complete human being?

Justice

- Who loves me?
- How do we know what's right?
- Who is my neighbour?

Forgiveness

- When should I say sorry?
- How do I say sorry?
- Why do I need to receive forgiveness?
- How do I know when I should forgive?
- What changes when you forgive?
- How do you forgive yourself?
- How do you know that you are forgiven?

Peace

- Where do I feel comfortable and at peace? Which people make me feel at peace?
- How can I resolve conflict?
- How can I bring peace to others?
- What does peace mean to me?
- What makes me feel peaceful?

- Can I contribute to a peaceful community?
- Are there 'stages' in peace: peace within yourself; peace with close family friends; peace within the school community; peace within the local community; peace within a nation; peace between nations?

Friendship

- What is a friend?
- Who are my friends?
- How do I show friendship to others?
- How do I make friends?
- Why do I need friends?
- When do friends fall out?
- How do I maintain a friendship?

Humility

- What do I like about myself?
- How do I recognise my gifts?
- How do I feel when others are good at things?
- How do I put others before myself?

Truth

- How do I know who to believe?
- How do I tell the truth?
- Should I always tell the truth?
- Do I always respond positively to hearing the truth?
- Is truth different to different people?

Thanks

- What should I be thankful for – about myself? About others?
- How do I show my appreciation of others and myself?
- How do we celebrate who we are?
- How do we celebrate change?
- Who should I be thankful for?
- How do we celebrate milestones in our lives?

Compassion

- How do I become friends with those who are different to me? In what ways are people different to one another?
- How can I become a good listener?
- When should I be compassionate towards others and myself?
- What is it I love about myself? Why should I love myself?
- Can you think of times when 'your heart has gone out to somebody'? Did you act on this feeling?

Hope

- What do I hope for?
- What makes me feel 'hopeless'?
- Where do I see hope in the world?
- Who gives me hope?
- What do others hope for?
- How can I give hope to others?

Wisdom

- What steps can I take to help me make wise decisions?
- Which decisions in life require the most wisdom?
- Who helps me make important decisions?

Endurance

- What things are worth working for/at– even if we don't see immediate results?
- What/who might inspire and encourage me when I face difficulties in life?

Service

- What are my special gifts?
- How can I use these gifts to serve others?
- Does serving others mean that (don't take care of yourself or that I never assert myself?

Reverence

- How do I show respect and reverence to others?
- In what practical ways could a husband and wife show respect and reverence to one another?
- How do I treat other people when I disagree with them?
- How do I show respect to others?
- Would spending time in quietness and reflection help me when I have to make important decisions?

Koinonia

- Who helps and supports me?
- Which communities do I belong to?
- Who might help me in the future?
- What gifts do I share in the communities to which I belong – e.g. school; faith community; family; friendship groups; clubs/groups to which I belong?

Appendix 2

Sex and Relationships Education policy for use in Church of England primary schools

This sample policy is based on SRE policy documents approved by Bristol and Salisbury diocesan boards of education for use in their church schools. It should be used as a template for the governing bodies of Church of England schools to discuss, amend and adopt, in the light of their unique school context. Following agreement on a school policy, it should be signed by the Chair of Governors. Notes to the policy are in italic text.

Sample Sex and Relationships Education policy

1 Introduction

1.1 This school's SRE policy is based on the DCSF's *Sex and Relationships Education Guidance.*

Sex education is part of the personal, social and health education curriculum in our school. We will teach within a framework of Christian values and the Christian understanding that sex is a gift of God as part of creation. Whilst we use sex education to inform children about sexual issues, we do this with regard to matters of morality and individual responsibility, and in a way that allows children to ask and explore moral questions. (We have taken account of the guidance provided in teaching materials supplied by the Diocese.) Sensitivity and respect should be shown to all children when teaching about personal relationships and sex education and SRE should be taught in a way to ensure that there is no stigmatization of children based on their home/personal circumstances.

1.2 Context

All SRE in a Church of England school should be set in a context which is consistent with the school's Christian ethos and values.

- SRE should be based on inclusive Christian principles and values, emphasising respect, compassion, loving care and forgiveness.

- SRE should be taught in the light of the belief in the absolute worth of all people and the unconditional infinite love of God.

- SRE should reflect that sex is a gift from God as part of creation: a human longing for an intimate union.

- SRE should be sensitive to the circumstances of all children and be mindful of the variety of expressions of family life in our culture, yet it should also uphold the Christian values regarding relationships and marriage.

73

- Issues regarding human sexuality should be addressed sensitively.

- The exploration of reproduction and sexual behaviour within the science curriculum should stand alongside the exploration of relationships, values and morals and Christian belief.

Whilst pupils are given the opportunity to explore their own attitudes, values and beliefs and to develop an individual moral code that will guide their actions, this is exercised within an understanding of the right of people to hold their own views within a framework of respect for others.

2   Aims and objectives

2.1 We teach children about:

- The physical development of their bodies as they grow into adults;
- The way humans reproduce;
- Respect for their own bodies and the importance of sexual activity as part of a committed, long-term and loving relationship;
- The importance of marriage and family life;
- Moral questions;
- Relationship issues;
- Respect for the views of other people;
- What they should do if they are worried about any sexual matters.

3   Principles

SRE should be based on the following principles:

- The sanctity of marriage is an important belief in Christian teaching and practice.
- Children should learn the significance of marriage and families as key building blocks of community and society.
- Sex education includes learning about physical and emotional development.
- Children will be taught the cultural and religious differences about matters of sexuality.
- Sex education is part of a wider social, personal, spiritual and moral education process.
- Children should be made aware of the way in which advertising and the media influences their views about sexuality.
- Children should be made more aware of the spiritual dimensions and joys of intimacy.
- Children should be taught to have respect for their own and other people's bodies.
- Children should learn about their responsibilities to others, and be aware of the consequences of sexual activity.
- Children should learn that some people choose not to engage in sexual activity and that this should be respected and valued as a response to the gift of faith.
- Children should be taught to understand the power of sexual desire.
- Children should be made aware that sex can be used compulsively, competitively and destructively.
- Children need to learn the importance of protecting themselves, and of self-control.
- Children should be made aware of God's forgiveness and that there is always a way back.
- Children should learn that it is important to build positive relationships that involve trust and respect.
- Children need to learn how to keep themselves safe when using the Internet and other forms of technology.
- Children need to be aware of responsible use of all forms of technology in order to respect the well-being and integrity of others.

4   The National Healthy School Standard

We now participate in the National Healthy School Standard scheme, which promotes health education. As participants in this scheme we:

- consult with parents on all matters of health education policy;
- train all our teachers to teach sex education;
- listen to the views of the children in our school regarding sex education;
- look positively at any local initiatives that support us in providing the best sex education teaching programme that we can devise.

5   Organisation

5.1   We teach sex education through different aspects of the curriculum. While we carry out the main sex education teaching in our Personal, Social, Health and Economic (PSHE) curriculum, we also teach some sex education through other subject areas (for example, in science, PE and RE), where we feel that they contribute significantly to a child's knowledge and understanding of his or her own body, and how it is changing and developing.

5.2   In PSHE education we teach children about relationships, and we encourage children to discuss issues. We teach about the parts of the body and how these work, and we explain to them what will happen to their bodies during puberty. For example, we tell the boys that their voices will change during puberty and we explain to the girls about menstruation. We encourage the children to ask for help if they need it.

5.3   In science lessons, in both key stages, teachers inform children about puberty and how a baby is born. For this aspect of the school's teaching, we follow the guidance material in the national scheme of work for science. In Key Stage 1 we teach children about how animals, including humans, move, feed, grow and reproduce, and we also teach them about the main parts of the body. Children learn to appreciate the differences between people and how to show respect for each other. In Key Stage 2 we teach about life processes and the main stages of the human life cycle in greater depth.

5.4   In Key Stage 2 RE children will learn about the commitment of people of faith to each other in marriage and how this is expressed in marriage ceremonies. They will learn about the beliefs and values that underpin this commitment and support the nurture and care of children in the family.

5.5   In years 5 and 6 we place a particular emphasis on health education, as many children experience the onset of puberty at this age. We liaise with the local health authority about suitable teaching materials to use with our children in these lessons. Teachers do their best to answer all questions with sensitivity and care. By the end of Key Stage 2, we ensure that both boys and girls know how babies are born, how their bodies change during puberty, what menstruation is, and how it affects women. We always teach this with due regard for the emotional development of the children (as stated earlier in this policy).

5.6   We arrange a meeting for all parents and carers of children in Year 6 to discuss this particular programme of lessons, to explain what the issues are and how they are taught, and to see the materials the school uses in its teaching.

6 The role of parents

6.1 The school is well aware that the primary role in children's sex education lies with parents and carers. We wish to build a positive and supportive relationship with the parents of children at our school through mutual understanding, trust and co-operation. In promoting this objective we:

- inform parents about the school's sex education policy and practice;
- answer any questions that parents may have about the sex education of their child;
- take seriously any issue that parents raise with teachers or governors about this policy or the arrangements for sex education in the school;
- inform parents about the teaching of sex education in school so that the parents and school can work together to support the child with regard to sex education. We believe that, through this mutual exchange of knowledge and information, children will benefit from being given consistent messages about their changing bodies and their increasing responsibilities.

6.2 Parents have the right to withdraw their child from all or part of the sex education programme that we teach in our school. If a parent wishes their child to be withdrawn from sex education lessons, they should discuss this with the headteacher, and make it clear which aspects of the programme they do not want their child to participate in. The school always complies with the wishes of parents in this regard.

7 The role of other members of the community

7.1 We encourage other valued members of the community to work with us to provide advice and support to the children with regard to health education. In particular, members of the Local Health Authority, such as the school nurse and other health professionals, give us valuable support with our sex education programme. Other people that we call on include local clergy, social workers and youth workers.

8 Confidentiality and safeguarding children procedures

8.1 Teachers conduct sex education lessons in a sensitive manner and in confidence. However, if a child makes a reference to being involved, or likely to be involved, in sexual activity, then the teacher will take the matter seriously and deal with it as a matter of child protection. Teachers will respond in a similar way if a child indicates that he/she may have been a victim of abuse. If the teachers have concerns, they will draw their concerns to the attention of the headteacher and/or the designated teacher for child protection and safeguarding. The headteacher will then deal with the matter in consultation with health care professionals. (See also Child Protection Policy.)

Advice for teachers on particularly sensitive issues such as female circumcision can be found at: http://www.teachernet.gov.uk/wholeschool/familyandcommunity/childprotection

9 The role of the headteacher

9.1 It is the responsibility of the headteacher to ensure that both staff and parents are informed about our sex education policy, and that the policy is implemented effectively. It is also the headteacher's responsibility to ensure that members of staff are given sufficient training, so that they can teach effectively and handle any difficult issues with sensitivity.

9.2 The headteacher liaises with external agencies regarding the school sex education programme, and ensures that all adults who work with children on these issues are aware of the school policy, and that they work within this framework.

9.3 The headteacher monitors this policy on a regular basis and reports to governors, when requested, on the effectiveness of the policy.

10 Monitoring and review

10.1 The Curriculum Committee of the governing body monitors our sex education policy on an annual basis. This committee reports its findings and recommendations to the full governing body, as necessary, if the policy needs modification. The Curriculum Committee gives serious consideration to any comments from parents about the sex education programme, and makes a record of all such comments. Governors require the headteacher to keep a written record, giving details of the content and delivery of the sex education programme that we teach in our school. Governors should scrutinise materials to check they are in accordance with the school's ethos.

10.2 The SRE Policy has clear links with other school policies aimed at promoting pupils' spiritual, moral, social and cultural development, including the:

Equal Opportunities Policy

Health and Safety Policy

Inclusion Policy

Special Educational Needs Policy

Drugs Education Policy

PSHE and Citizenship Policy

Behaviour Policy

Anti-bullying Policy

Safeguarding/Child Protection Policy

ICT Policy and Safe Internet Use Policy

Confidentiality Policy

Signed:

Date:

SRE Policy: points to consider for staff and governors

Sex and Relationships Education in C of E Primary Schools

The DCSF Sex and Relationship Education guidance states that Sex and Relationship Education (SRE) should be firmly rooted within the framework for Personal, Social, Health and Economic (PSHE) education and Citizenship. However, questions have been raised about how sex education should be taught within a Church School setting – reflecting both the distinctive ethos and values which underpin a Church School. In response to these issues, the following guidance is offered to facilitate discussion when developing a policy.

Context

- SRE should be based on inclusive Christian principles and values, emphasising respect, compassion, loving care and forgiveness.
- SRE should be taught in the light of the belief in the absolute worth of all persons and the unconditional infinite love of God.
- SRE should reflect that sex is a gift from God as part of creation: a human longing for an intimate union.
- SRE should be sensitive to the circumstances of all children and be mindful of the variety of expressions of family life in our culture, yet it should also uphold the Christian values regarding relationships and marriage.

Guiding principles

In a Church of England school Christian beliefs and values should underpin SRE such that SRE is taught in the belief that:

- The sanctity of marriage is an important belief in Christian teaching and practice.
- Children should learn the significance of marriage and families as key building blocks of community and society.
- Sex education includes learning about physical and emotional development.
- Sex education is part of a wider social, personal, spiritual and moral education process.
- Children should be made aware of the way in which advertising and the media influences their views about sexuality.
- Children should be taught to have respect for their own and other people's bodies.
- Children should be taught to understand the power of sexual desire.
- Children should be made more aware of the spiritual dimensions and joys of intimacy.
- Children should learn about their responsibilities to others, and be aware of the consequences of sexual activity.
- Children should be guided to understand the importance of building positive relationships that involve trust and respect.
- Children should be made aware that sex can be used compulsively, competitively and destructively.
- Children should be made aware of God's forgiveness and that there is always a way back.
- Children need to learn the importance of protecting themselves and of self control.
- Children will be taught the cultural and religious differences about matters of sexuality.
- Children should learn that some people choose not to engage in sexual activity and that this should be respected and valued as a response to the gift of faith.
- Children need to learn how to keep themselves safe when using the Internet and other forms of technology.
- Children need to be aware of responsible use of all forms of technology in order to respect the wellbeing and integrity of others.

Role of parents

The primary role in children's sex education lies with parents and carers. It is therefore important to build positive and supportive relationships with the parents and carers through mutual understanding, trust and co-operation.

Role of the local church and community

Members of the local health authority, such as the school nurse and other health professionals, are available to give support. In addition, the local church community can be a valuable resource in teaching about Christian marriage.

Role of the headteacher and governors

In a VA school the responsibility for the SRE policy lies with the governors. The headteacher has to ensure that both staff and parents are informed about the school's sex education policy, and that the policy is implemented effectively. The governing body should carefully scrutinise teaching material to ensure it is appropriate for the school's distinctive ethos and foundation and that it is age appropriate.

Confidentiality and safeguarding children procedures

Due regard should be given to Child Protection Policy in the development and delivery of SRE.

Questions to facilitate discussion

- How do we respect a wide range of individual beliefs and practices whilst upholding the Christian ideal of the sanctity of marriage?
- How can we equip children to deal with the challenges of peer pressure?
- How can we enable children to recognise that substances, such as alcohol or drugs, impede self-control and lead to actions which may later be regretted? How do we help children to explore the importance of self-control in their lives?
- In order to develop a healthy sexual relationship in later life, children need to develop positive relationships, involving trust and respect. How do we help children to develop the skills necessary to achieve this?
- How do we help our children to protect themselves against sexual exploitation?
- How can the local church community be used as a resource for teaching about Christian marriage?
- What procedures are in place to monitor the governing body and headteacher's responsibilities for SRE?
- What provision do we make to encourage safe and responsible use of the Internet?

Appendix

Sex and Relationships Education: Working with parents

The DCSF guidelines for Sex and Relationships Education (SRE) state that: 'Schools should always seek to work in partnership with parents. This is essential to effective sex and relationships education.'[11]

Parents play a crucial role in educating their children about sex and relationships and also in helping them navigate the emotional and physical aspects of puberty. Through conversations, family ethos and the broad approach to life, young people pick up a significant amount of information about relationships from their parents. Despite this, many parents find it hard to talk to their children openly about sex and relationships. Schools are strongly encouraged to support parents in the important role they play, creating opportunity for discussion about the SRE curriculum and its implementation. It is important for parents to feel comfortable with a school's proposed SRE teaching and policy so that they are able to support their children in this aspect of their learning.

Currently, parents still have the right to withdraw their children from SRE lessons taught as part of the PSHE education and Citizenship curriculum, though only a very small minority choose to do so. If a parent is concerned about SRE, arranging a meeting with them where they can discuss their concerns can be helpful.

Ideas for connecting with parents

There are numerous ways of connecting with parents before SRE lessons begin. Overleaf are a sample letter explaining this course and a suggested outline for a parents' evening. There is also a list of useful resources for parents, which can be downloaded from the Internet. It is suggested that parents are contacted well before the lessons begin to give them ample time to respond and build support for the course.

Parents' SRE letter

A good letter might include the following information:
- which topics will be covered in which weeks so that parents can follow specific issues up at home;
- an explanation of the theology and philosophy behind the course;
- a recognition of the important role that parents play in SRE;
- an invitation to a parents' evening before the beginning of SRE lessons if appropriate.

Overleaf is a sample letter that might be sent to parents:

---

11. Department for Education and Employment, *Sex and Relationships Education Guidance* (0116-200) (DfEE, London, 2000), pp.25–26. Also see DCSF, *Sex and Relationships Education Guidance 2010* (forthcoming).

[Date]

Dear

I am writing to inform you about the Sex and Relationships Education (SRE) that [Year 5] will receive during the [summer term] as part of their Personal, Social, Health and Economic (PSHE) education and Citizenship curriculum.

Every class will have three SRE lessons, during which pupils will have the chance to explore aspects of sex and relationships. The first lesson, 'Making me', looks at identity and what makes a person valuable. The second lesson, 'My world, your world', will allow the children to think about how good decisions can be made, with a greater awareness of the possible outcomes. The final lesson, 'Great expectations?', allows pupils to consider what they think about sex, and explores the opinions of different faiths on the significance of sex.

These lessons come from *Love and Sex Matters,* a new resource that has been produced with church schools in mind. It aims to give children and young people a safe environment within which they can explore different perspectives on sex and relationships.

The lessons present children with a variety of religious and non-religious viewpoints to allow them to make more considered decisions for themselves as they enter adolescence. The resources also allow children to assess critically the messages they receive from media and advertising. They encourage children to develop language suitable to discuss these often difficult subjects. The resources place a strong emphasis on the fact that healthy relationships are based upon people valuing both themselves, and other people.

We recognise that SRE can cause some parents concern. We also recognise that parents have an important role in teaching their children about sex and relationships, though many find it hard to talk openly about this area. We would like to invite you to a parents' SRE evening on [date], when we will explain in detail the school's policy on SRE and the curriculum we are using. There will be the opportunity for parents to ask questions and share their own perspectives. We do hope you will be able to attend this evening and actively support your children as they undertake SRE.

Yours sincerely,

[Name]

Parents' SRE meeting

Below is a suggested outline for an hour-long parents' meeting about the SRE curriculum.

Welcome (5 minutes)

It might be a good idea to start the evening off with some facts about what young people think about SRE or a funny film clip, e.g.:

- *SRE: Are You Getting It?* (London, UK Youth Parliament), see www.ukyouthparliament.org.uk. A recent survey of young people's views of SRE.
- Excerpt from *Angus, Thongs and Perfect Snogging*; the first five minutes of the film has a comical scene between two parents and their teenage daughter.
- *Vox Pop on Love and Sex,* www.truetube.co.uk
- One of the numerous clips on BBC Bare Facts, where children give their opinion on how and when parents should discuss sex, www.bbc.co.uk/barefacts

Small group discussion (15 minutes)

Ask parents, in small groups, to discuss the following two questions:

- What do you think SRE should cover?
- Do you think that parents have an important role in SRE?

Ask some of the groups to share the outcome of their discussions.

Presentation (15 minutes)

- Explanation of the school's SRE policy and SRE values framework (N.B. depending on the demographic of your school, it may also help to explain briefly a [the] Christian perspective[s] on sex.)
- Explanation of the theology and philosophy of this course as outlined in the introduction.
- Explanation of the important role parents play in SRE as outlined above.
- Explain and present one of the activities taken from *Love and Sex Matters* (for example the card sorting from the summary activities).
- Tips for talking to children about sex and relationships (*Talk to Your Children About Sex and Relationships: Support for Parents* has some good guidelines – see below).

Question time (20 minutes)

- Invite parents to share any concerns they have with aspects of the policy, values or curriculum.
- Invite any further questions.

Resources for parents

There are leaflets for parents about SRE available for free download on the Internet (see below). It is also good to give parents a copy of the school's SRE policy and SRE values Internet, so that they understand why SRE is taught as it is and are able to provide support as they feel is appropriate.

SRE & Parents Leaflet (0706 2001) (Department for Education and Skills, 2001), available at www.teachernet.gov.uk

Talk to Your Children About Sex and Relationships: Support for Parents (National Children's Bureau, 2003), available at www.ncb.org.uk

The NHS website has some guidance on talking to your children about sex, see http://www.nhs.uk/Livewell/Sexualhealth/Pages/Talktoyourteen.aspx or http://www.nhs.uk/chq/Pages/2341.aspx?CategoryID=62&SubCategoryID=66

The BBC website also has a section dedicated to helping parents talk to their children about sex, see www.bbc.co.uk/barefacts

Bibliography and further resources

Books and articles

Arnold, Johann Christoph, *A Plea for Purity: Sex, Marriage and God* (Plough Publishing House: New York, 1998)

Bell, Rob, *Sex God* (Zondervan: Michigan, 2007)

Brandon, Guy, *Just Sex* (Inter-Varsity Press: Nottingham, 2009)

Dunn, Judy & Layard, Richard, *A Good Childhood: Searching for Values in a Competitive Age* (The Children's Society: London, 2009)

Ecclestone, Alan, *Yes to God* (Darton, Longman & Todd Ltd: London, 1975)

Highton, Mike, *Difficult Gospel: The Theology of Rowan Williams* (SCM Press: Canterbury, 2004)

Kilbourne, Jean, 'Beauty … and the Beast of Advertising', *Media & Values* (No.49, winter 1990), available at www.medialit.org/reading_room/article40.html

Sheldrake, Philip, *Befriending Our Desires* (Darton, Longman & Todd Ltd: London, 2002)

Williams, Rowan, *Lost Icons* (Continuum International Publishing Group Ltd: London, 2003)

Reports

Department for Education and Employment (now the DCSF), *Sex and Relationship Education Guidance* (0116-200), (DfEE, London, 2000)

House of Bishops' Group on Issues in Human Sexuality, *Some Issues in Human Sexuality: A Guide to the Debate* (Church House Publishing, London, 2003)

Macdonald, Sir Alasdair, *Independent Review of the Proposal to Make Personal, Social, Health and Economic (PSHE) Education Statutory* (Department for Children, Schools and Families (DCSF), London, 2009)

Teaching resources

Hope's Place has produced an eight-week course on self esteem for young women, Crowther, Joanna & Thomas, Elizabeth, *New I.D.* (2008), and a six-week course on identity for young men, Guthrie, Kate & Thomas, Dylan, *Man Up* (2009). See www.hopesplace.org.uk for more information.

Channel Four have a *Living and Growing DVD*, which many schools use as the basis of their PSHE education teaching.

Lovewise has a series of presentations on issues relating to SRE: *Choosing the Best, Growing Up … Growing Wise and Emotional and Physical*. See www.lovewise.org.uk for more information.

St Edward's RC School, Lees, Oldham, has developed an SRE resource for primary-aged children called *In the Beginning*. For more information, see the school website: www.st-edwards.oldham.sch.uk

Christian Action Research and Education send trained presenters into secondary schools to lead presentations. The programme is called *Evaluate: Informing Choice*. See www.evaluate.org.uk

Websites

www.4yp.co.uk
www.4ypbristol.co.uk
www.onesuffolk.co.uk/4yp
Websites for 4YP – sexual health and contraception services – for young people in Haringey, Bristol and Suffolk.

www.avert.org
Website of the charity Avert, an international AIDS charity, providing information about HIV and AIDS.

www.bbc.co.uk/religion
The BBC's webpages on religion.

www.bbc.co.uk/schools/gcsebitesize
The BBC's webpages on GCSEs; there is some useful information on religion and sex/relationships.

www.bbc.co.uk/barefacts
The BBC's webpages on talking to children about sex, love and relationships.

www.biblegateway.com
Website offering free access to many different versions and translations of the Bible.

www.brook.org.uk/
Website for Brook, which provides confidential sexual health advice for the under 25s.

www.checkyourbits.org
NHS website about STIs aimed at under-25s.

www.ChildLine.org.uk
Website of the counselling service for children, Childline.

www.drinkaware.co.uk
Website of the charity Drinkaware, providing information on alcohol, its effect on relationships, and on talking to under-18s about alcohol.

www.fpa.org.uk
Website of the sexual health charity FPA, which provides information, advice and support to people across the UK on all aspects of sexual health.

www.healthyschools.gov.uk
Website of government initiative The Healthy Schools Programme.

www.kidshealth.org
Website created by Nemours, a non-profit organization, providing information for children, teens and parents on all aspects health including sexual health.

www.nationalstrategies.standards.dcsf.gov.uk
National Strategies website from the DCSF.

www.ncb.org.uk
Website of the charity National Children's Bureau.

www.nhs.uk
The National Health Service website with information on living healthily, including sexual health.

www.pshe-cpd.com
Website of the PSHE CPD programme for teachers and community nurses.

www.romanceacademy.org
The website for Romance Academy, which is a 12–15 week project supporting and mentoring up to twelve young people as they build their self-esteem, enhanced by sexual delay.

www.tcwp.co.uk
Website of the Christopher Winter Project, a training and consultancy company that provide sex and relationships education to young people, and training for teachers.

www.teachernet.gov.uk
Website for teachers and school managers.

www.truetube.co.uk
Website run by the charity CTVC providing and hosting media and text created by young people on a range of different topics to help start debates.

www.yourchurchwedding.org
The Church of England website about planning a church wedding.